Foreword

Dr. Elaine Margarita and I have been colleagues and friends for many years. Despite our differences in age and experience, we share a mutual respect for each other and a love for our profession. We strongly believe that knowing another language and culture should be an essential part of every child's education, that ALL students can learn, and that an early start and a long sequence are essential to achieve a useful level of proficiency in a language. Our beliefs are echoed in all that we do, say, and write.

Elaine teaches the New York State approved FLES methods course for license extension K-6 on Long Island, as I do in Westchester County. We have shared ideas, materials, and examples to help enhance both of our courses and for the benefit of our college students. This book is a testament to Elaine's knowledge and research into the field of Early Foreign Language Instruction. It is both scholarly and practical and represents a major new resource on the cutting edge in foreign language education. It will become required reading in all my future classes, a reference item in all my FLES workshops, and a source of information for all those interested in exploring and implementing a FLES program in their schools.

I am very proud of Elaine and delighted to have had a hand in developing this very special book.

Harriet Schottland Barnett, Consultant, ACTFL (American Council on the Teaching of Foreign Languages)

Based on her doctoral studies and years of experience in the field of foreign language education at all levels of instruction, Dr. Elaine Margarita has devised an analytical and systematic approach for school districts to take as they seek to establish an elementary school foreign language program. While this manual describes the various forms that such a program could take (FLES, FLEX, Immersion), Dr. Margarita clearly and convincingly argues for the establishment of the ideal Sequential FLES program, one consisting of 18 components. Her arguments for foreign language study, in general, and FLES in particular, are based on various studies found in the literature and on interviews with FLES teachers, elementary school classroom teachers, administrators and parents.

In leading us to a policy position, vis-à-vis foreign language study in the elementary school, Dr. Margarita addresses the benefits and successes of such a program for students of all abilities; and its link to enhanced basic and cognitive skills, as well as the joy that comes from knowing another language. She lists the obstacles to the establishment of such a program and suggests how these obstacles can be overcome. While providing evidence for academic, cross-cultural, political, and social advantages to the establishment of a long term foreign language program beginning in the elementary school, Dr. Margarita points us to the need for further study and identifies specific areas. Dr. Margarita's manual is truly a unique document. It provides a process and a means by which we can reach a goal as it encourages further study in the field. Dr. Margarita's work clearly establishes her as a visionary educator in the field of foreign language instruction.

John La Monica, Former Chairperson, Foreign Languages, Syosset Schools

Preface

Situating Myself in the Work: A Note from the Author

I began this journey in January 1997, when I developed a course to certify

secondary teachers to teach foreign languages at the elementary school level (FLES).

Since the number of FLES programs on Long Island, New York was growing, more

teachers were needed who had this certification, and the coursework required for

certification by the New York State Department of Education was not offered at any local

college or university. As an Associate Professor of methodology for second languages at

Dowling College, I had the necessary background. In addition, I was in the second year

of my doctoral studies at Hofstra University. The course received approval from the New

York State Education Department and was offered in collaboration with the Dowling

Institute. I decided my dissertation topic would deal with foreign language programs at

the elementary school level.

In a discussion with my dissertation chair, Dr. Charol Shakeshaft, we realized I

was working towards embarking on an alternative form of dissertation: The Policy or

Advocacy Document. I had read about this alternative dissertation in one of my courses

in a paper written by a Hofstra professor, Dr. Lesley Browder. It certainly suited my

needs and interests. I also believed a policy document would assist local school districts,

as more and more were considering early foreign language programs.

The work progressed rapidly for me from there. I was able to build a knowledge

base through my studies and my experiences with teachers in the FLES Certification

Course. I also began presenting on this topic at state and local conferences, consulting at

school districts throughout Long Island, and interviewing educators from thirteen school districts on Long Island where early foreign language programs were starting in Kindergarten, first or second grade. The results of this work are presented in this policy document. The work includes a critical review of quantitative and qualitative studies, analyses of implementation issues (educational, economic, political, and social), a qualitative examination of the implementation experience for educators on Long Island, and a synthesis of relevant literature.

So, why should anyone listen to my efforts to advocate for early foreign language study? I taught Spanish for ten years. I am a coordinator for a K-12 world language program at a school district on Long Island. This policy would certainly serve my own interests. It preserves jobs for my colleagues and affirms my career choice. But, my vision goes past my job. It is a vision that is shared by many other educators, not all of whom are second language teachers. I believe all students can learn. I also believe all students can (and should) learn another language. I believe through this experience, students gain the confidence that comes with enhanced communication skills; they gain sensitivity towards "others." They experience joy. I have witnessed all this with my own students.

This policy may be seen by some as an attempt to satisfy certain groups. I believe it is another door we can open for our children, especially when other doors may be closing. On the other side of this door may be more solutions to the challenges of tomorrow. With this reflection, I begin.

Acknowledgements

I would like to express my appreciation to the many people who assisted me in producing this document. First, I thank Dr. Charol Shakeshaft. As a chair, a visionary, a leader, a scholar, and a mentor, Charol has been more than any one person could ask for in this rigorous process. I thank Dr. Bob Kottkamp, for always "putting the bar high" and for being there with a safety net of knowledge and wisdom if I fell. Sincere thanks are owed to Dr. Nancy Cloud, for her perfect vision of what was truly important. I also felt honored to have the insights of Dr. Timothy Smith and Dr. Joan Zaleski in this process.

To all the "leaders in the field" who became my guiding light and endless source of knowledge (Harriet Barnett, Helena Curtain, Carol Ann Pesola-Dahlberg, Mari Haas, Audrey Heining-Boynton, Gladys Lipton, Al Martino, Mimi Met, and Nancy Rhodes), thank you for all your exceptional work and willingness to share. I owe much of the success of this document to all the teachers, administrators, and colleagues who participated in the interviews, provided data, and were always willing to give more when asked (especially Mary Kenny, Josephine Maietta, Diane McLoughlin, Mary Jane McMaster, and Eglal Nasser).

Several special friends and colleagues were incredibly supportive. Harriet Barnett and Charlotte Rosenzweig gave hours and hours of reading, editing, and discussion time to help me frame this document into what it needed to be. I could not have believed in myself without my life-long best friends, Linda Ehrler-Kotch and Irene Lutchen-Berner, reminding me that I could do this. Your love and friendship is a special gift. To Marge Clark, Tania Johnson, John La Monica, and all my friends and colleagues at work, you know how important your support was, I thank you. To Nancy Rosenbluth, my research assistant and dear friend, and my niece, Marissa Ramirez, I thank you for the hours of data collection, your love, and dedication.

To my father and mother, I could never even recognize a rose, let alone be able to enjoy the beauty of its smell, without you. You put me on the path to succeed by setting an example and you provided endless nurturing and loving along the way. To my sisters, Elizabeth, Elvira, Elisa, and Ellen, you helped to raise my children, to work through the technology, to assuage my fears, and to bring me through the overwhelming moments. I could never thank you enough.

Finally, to my husband, Rich, the years of dedication you gave to me, to the dream I had, and to our children, are a testimony to the loving and generous spirit you are. I am eternally grateful.

Dedication

This work is dedicated to my three daughters, Sarabeth, Emily, and Julia.

Any dream or vision you have is possible. I love you way up past the sky.

To Nancy: Everything's coming up roses.

Terminology Used

Foreign language and **Second language** are used interchangeably throughout the paper. While the terms **Languages Other Than English** (LOTE) or **World Languages** are more appropriate in today's context, the majority of the literature reviewed and people interviewed used the former expressions. In an effort to maintain consistency and cohesiveness in the document, "foreign" and "second" language are used.

FLES stands for foreign languages in the elementary school or foreign languages, early start. It is often used in the literature as an umbrella term for all forms of early foreign language programs, in addition to referring to a specific model. The (Sequential) FLES model is the targeted model for this document.

Language-minority students are individuals who come from a minority group. Their first language is not English.

Language-majority students are individuals whose first language is English.

Proficiency is defined by the American Council on the Teaching of Foreign Languages (ACTFL) as how well an individual functions in the language in terms of comprehensibility, comprehension, language control, vocabulary, cultural awareness, and communication strategies (ACTFL, 1999).

Communicative competence is the ability to recognize and produce language correctly, idiomatically, fluently, and appropriately in a variety of communicative settings. It includes grammatical competence, sociolinguistic competence, discourse competence, and strategic competence in speech and in writing.

Table of Contents

Tables

Appendices

Section One

Introduction

Across the nation, the percentage of elementary schools offering foreign language instruction has risen almost ten percent over the last ten years from 22% to 31% (Branaman & Rhodes, 1997). "Despite these positive trends, there is still reason for concern about the limited number of K-12 long-sequence language programs that are designed to educate students linguistically and culturally to communicate successfully in the U.S. and abroad (Branaman & Rhodes, 1997, p. 6)."

There is considerable evidence to justify an early start for foreign language instruction. Brain studies and psycholinguistic literature support the argument that language acquisition is best achieved when started at a young age (Nash, 1997; Newport, 1990). As the child ages, the brain loses its "plasticity." This plasticity is one of the features required for fluent acquisition of a second language (Lenneberg, 1967; Winslow, 1997).

Curtain and Pesola (1994) presented a three-pronged argument for the implementation of foreign languages in the elementary schools. First, beginning foreign languages at the elementary school level increases the time allowed for practice and experience that is crucial to language learning. Second, since studies show ten is a crucial age for attitude development (Lambert & Klineberg, 1967), global awareness and sensitivity to others are best developed in children under age ten. Third, all subject areas of importance to our educational system (math, science, social studies, art, health, etc.) are introduced in the elementary curricula. If learning a foreign language is a goal of our educational system, then implementing foreign languages in the early elementary school grades is essential (Curtain & Pesola, 1994, pp. 3-4).

When parents, boards of education, administrators, and teachers discuss a policy of early second language study, some of the issues that arise are: finding time in the school day, funding, deciding which language(s) to offer, and staffing. These issues need consideration in the decision-making process towards implementing a policy of foreign language study at the elementary school level. One of the first implementation decisions is the model chosen.

There are four primary models for foreign language study at the elementary school level (FLES):

- **FLEX** or Foreign Language Exploratory/Experience/Exposure programs offer exposure to more than one language for a limited time with a focus on cultural awareness and minimal language proficiency expected.

- **Sequential FLES** (also referred to in this document as **FLES**) or Foreign Languages at the Elementary School programs offer sequential instruction in one language for two or more years with a degree of language proficiency and cultural awareness expected.

- **Immersion** programs offer 50% -100% of the school day conducted in the target language with a substantial degree of fluency and cultural awareness expected after four years.

- **Dual immersion** programs resemble immersion programs but serve language-minority and language-majority students in the same classrooms and aim for bilingualism and biculturalism for both groups of students.

(The term **FLES** is also used as an umbrella term for all types of foreign language study at the elementary school level.) The outcomes of each model depend greatly on the design of implementation. Obviously, the greater the amount of time provided in the target language, the greater the expected proficiency (Curtain, 1993; Heining-Boynton, 1998).

The Sequential FLES and immersion models are the most effective for developing second language proficiency (Rhodes et al., 1989). The immersion models are most likely to be implemented in a school district with a large population of language-minority students (children whose first language is not English) or where there is a great degree of community support for an immersion program.

In many of our schools, it is expected that the language-minority student will become bilingual, but it is not expected that the language-majority student will also become bilingual. Given the multicultural reality of our schools and communities, schools are forced to respond to the needs of the language-minority child to help him or her to become proficient in another language. However, there is no corresponding impetus for the language-majority child who must also face future realities. This policy document focuses on the needs of language-majority children, since it is equally important to address their needs in our diverse society. The model advocated by this document (Sequential FLES) may easily be provided to language-majority children.

The FLEX model has advantages in terms of the diversity of languages and cultural exposure, yet it is too limited in its expected outcomes for language proficiency. Immersion has programmatic and staffing requirements, and must have strong community and administrative support. Dual immersion is like immersion, except there is the added requirement of having enough language-minority children in the school population. The FLES model is a "gateway" program for districts to consider. It is a model that any district should be able to implement. While the immersion models would provide the best environment for language proficiency, the additional requirements may not make them as viable as the FLES model. For these reasons, this document advocates for the implementation of the FLES model.

In advocating for the FLES model, this document is not proposing to eliminate consideration of the immersion models. On the contrary, wherever the interest and conditions allow, immersion should be explored since it is truly the ideal program for developing language proficiency and cultural sensitivity. Immersion programs have met with great success in many school districts throughout the nation.

Purpose

This advocacy document examines and argues for implementation of early-start, sequential foreign languages programs (FLES) in public elementary schools, grades K-6. Policy development in private or independent schools is very distinct from the public school experience and, in particular, policy for foreign language study varies a great deal from one independent school to another. This document focuses on the implications of implementing FLES programs in public school districts where there currently is no foreign language elementary program and where FLES would most likely be the model chosen.

To develop this advocacy position I: (1) provide a research-based rationale for FLES, (2) describe an "Ideal FLES Model," (3) present argumentation for the FLES model and its 18 components, (4) examine the effects of a FLES program based on research, (5) discuss obstacles and challenges to implementing a FLES program, and (6) consider a range of organizational and environmental (educational, economic, political, and social) factors that contribute to the successful implementation of FLES. The Ideal FLES Model is based on research studies, the literature on FLES, data on current programs, and the interviews conducted for this analysis.

This document is divided into fifteen sections. The first section, the Introduction, is followed by Section Two, the Background, which sets this policy in national, state, and local contexts. A rationale for early second language study is presented in Section Three. The argumentation for adopting a FLES program is presented in Section Four. The "Ideal FLES Model" is described in Section Five. Section Six provides the argumentation for the Ideal Model and its 18 components. Section Seven includes a discussion of the effects of FLES programs based on evidence found in research. In Section Eight, the obstacles or challenges to implementation are discussed. Section Nine includes a discussion of political and social issues. Sections Ten through Fourteen provide specific guidelines around implementation issues (beginning the process, presenting to the board, child development issues, curriculum, and assessment). These sections are also designed to facilitate discussion in methodology courses. Section Fifteen provides summaries of the previous sections and offers some conclusions and suggested research.

In addition to research studies and related literature on FLES, this document includes data collected through interviews of personnel from twenty school districts on Long Island, New York (13 with Sequential FLES programs and 7 without, see Appendix

A), officials from the New York State Education Department, and leaders in the field of second language study. The studies reviewed and interviews conducted are based on Sequential FLES programs for language-majority students (students whose first language is English), unless otherwise stated. School districts with FLEX or immersion models are not part of the analysis. (Data were also collected on school districts throughout Long Island, New York to determine how many districts begin foreign language study before grade 7. This information is presented in Appendix B. A summary of these two Appendices is provided at the end of Appendix B.). Critical reviews are presented of the most recent studies available (from the 1980s and 1990s). Earlier studies are included in the review if they are noted for their implications and strength of design.

Section Two

Background: The History and Status of FLES Policy

This section of the document includes a discussion of the current status of early second language policy from a national, state, and local perspective. It begins by setting the policy in an historical context. The discussion that follows highlights the national, state, and local initiatives that support this policy.

The Current Context. Support for a policy of foreign languages at the elementary school level (FLES) is inextricably linked to political, economic, social, and, educational contexts (Phillips, 1994; Ramirez, 1998). Federal and local governments have increasingly supported policies of FLES over the last 10 years. Historically, national and local support for FLES programs has come on the heels of federal or state reports, memoranda, or initiatives. The most recent initiatives (Educate America 2000, The National Standards for Foreign Language Learning, The Report of the New York State Foreign Language Implementation Committee, The New York State Framework for Languages Other Than English [LOTE], Educating America's Children for Tomorrow Act of 1998, Educational Excellence for All Children Act of 1999) document our lack of competitiveness with other nations in the area of linguistic and cross-cultural competence and/or cite the elementary school as the optimal starting point for addressing this problem.

Why would federal and state agencies support early foreign language learning? "International trade…now represents a major force. Domestically, …businesses as well as public and social service organizations are rapidly adjusting to the demand for products and services accessed in a wide range of languages" (Brecht & Walton, 1995, p.110). Our communities are becoming microcosms of the world-at-large. These

initiatives support the belief that language is the means for building connections with

others both within our communities and beyond our borders (Wing, 1996).

More importantly, recent world events have brought our nation to the realization

that our children need to develop an understanding of and sensitivity towards other

cultures. After the crisis of September 11, 2001, New York State's Commissioner of

Education addressed district superintendents in a letter, stating, "one of the key issues

schools are facing [is] the need to promote tolerance and to make students of all races,

religions, and national origins feel safe and respected in school (Mills, 10/04/01)." A

FLES program is an investment in the effort to develop this tolerance.

In the 1960s, school districts around the country implemented FLES programs in

an effort to improve our ability to respond to world events. "Public awareness of the

value of foreign language education was heightened by the jarring information that the

United States could have known about the development of the Russian satellite (Sputnik)

had American scientists been regular readers of Russian journals" (Curtain & Pesola,

1994, p. 16). The quick response was philosophically sound, but the implementation

procedures were not carefully thought out. Most of these programs were short-lived.

They suffered from a lack of clear objectives, poor planning, limited resources, poorly

prepared teachers, a lack of articulation plans with secondary programs, and an absence

of plans for program evaluation (Alkonis & Brophy, 1961). Policymakers for today's

second language programs have research on second language acquisition and the results

of second language programs in formal school settings to guide and inform them as they

plan for challenging and successful programs (Curtain & Pesola, 1994).

As the new millennium is upon us, the nation has again focused on the need to maintain a global agenda. The media, federal, and state reports constantly compare our performance to the performance of students in neighboring communities and in schools around the world. They also demonstrate how the world is becoming part of our own communities.

> Congress finds that…even though all residents of the United States
>
> should be proficient in English, without regard to their country of
>
> birth, it is also of vital importance to the competitiveness of the
>
> United States that those residents be encouraged to learn other
>
> languages…(Educating America's Children for Tomorrow Act, S.667, Section
>
> 402, November, 1998).

United States Secretary of Education Richard W. Riley gave a statement regarding the legislative act entitled, The Education Excellence for All Children Act of 1999.

> The number of public elementary schools teaching foreign languages has
>
> grown quickly over the past ten years. However, only a small percentage of
>
> our elementary schools are teaching foreign languages in a manner that will
>
> develop proficiency in a second language….The legislation would set a
>
> National goal that, by 2005, 25 percent of America's elementary schools will
>
> have foreign language programs that focus on attaining language proficiency
>
> and are well coordinated with middle and secondary school programs (United
>
> States Secretary of Education, Richard Riley, February 11, 1999).

The International Context. Globally, foreign language programs, such as FLES, have been implemented at the primary level. Four countries in Europe (Denmark, the

Netherlands, Belgium, and Luxembourg) currently have compulsory foreign language study at the primary level and several other countries (France, Greece, Italy, Spain, and Scotland) have introduced educational reforms that include FLES. In Great Britain and Russia, all students begin the study of a second language by grade 5. In Germany, foreign language usually begins in grade three and there are some experimental programs beginning earlier. Israeli children begin the study of a second language in grade four. In Egypt, the study of a second language begins in first grade.

Most of the Canadian provinces offer foreign language instruction (immersion) in the early primary grades. A majority of the Australian states are making the study of a second language at the elementary level compulsory. Students in Finland, Hungary, Norway, and Sweden all begin study of a second language by grade four, some beginning as early as second grade. Austrian students begin by third grade, with some experimental schools starting in Kindergarten or first grade (Bergentoft, 1994; Curtain, 1999, New York State Association of Foreign Language Teachers, 1999; Rosenbusch, 1995). Clearly, the advancement of the instruction of foreign languages at the primary level has received higher priority in other nations at greater levels than in the United States (see summary chart from Pufahl, Rhodes, & Christian, 2000, Appendix D).

Traditionally, the United States has never been competitive in its development of standards for foreign language learning (Munks, 1996; Rosenbusch, 1995). In recent years, however, policymakers have taken steps to address this failing (Met, 1998; Rosenbusch, 1995). The current momentum that started the direction of advocacy for this policy is found in the Educate America 2000 legislation with a goal of second language proficiency for all students.

I believe that America's children need to become much more fluent in other

languages. We are very behind other nations when it comes to giving our

students a mastery of other languages. I am certain we can do a much better job

of giving our students both a mastery of English and fluency in at least one

foreign language (United States Secretary of Education, Richard W. Riley,

February 11, 1999).

National and State Initiatives. On the national level, legislators have recently introduced

and passed initiatives promoting foreign language study at an early age. Educate

America 2000 legislation is an attempt to reform and improve national curricula, with

foreign languages acknowledged as part of the nation's goals. National Education Goal

#3 (Student Achievement and Citizenship) states, "All students will leave grades 4, 8, and

12 having demonstrated competency over challenging subject matter including…foreign

languages" (National Education Goals, 1995, p. 2).

Leaders in the field of second language education have developed the national

standards (National Standards for Foreign Language Education, 1996, see Appendix C)

along with standards for all core subject areas. These standards "support the ideal of

extended sequences of study that begin in the elementary grades and continue through

high school and beyond" (National Standards Executive Summary, 1996, p. 1). In

November, 1998, the Senate passed the Educating America's Children for Tomorrow Act

(S. 667) which mandates the study of how multilingual we are as a nation in an effort to

develop innovative initiatives to promote the importance of foreign language skills.

At the writing of this document, eight states mandate programs in languages other

than English beginning in the elementary school (Arizona, Arkansas, Louisiana,

Massachusetts, Montana, New Jersey, North Carolina, and Oklahoma). New York currently has a requirement for two years of study of a second language at some point between grades K-9 (New York State Regents Graduation Requirements, 1998). A mandate for an early start for second language education in New York State has often been an item of discussion.

In supporting FLES and the National Standards, The New York State Framework for Languages Other Than English (LOTE) stated, "to achieve the language competencies of the performance indicators in this Framework, students need opportunities to begin the study of a language other than English in elementary school and to continue that study in a sequential, developmental program through secondary school" (p. 4). In 1997, the Commissioner of Education in New York State appointed a Foreign Language Implementation Committee to analyze and make recommendations regarding increased requirements for second language study. This committee recommended that all school districts offer foreign languages at the elementary school level (New York State Foreign Language Implementation Committee, 1998).

The Local Context. What is the history of this policy on Long Island? One school district on Long Island has maintained a FLES program since 1965. Another district started a program in the late 1980s. Currently, throughout Long Island, there is an increased interest in school districts to examine the implementation of FLES programs. (The number of dual immersion programs has also increased, as districts are responding to the needs and interests of their communities.) During the 1990s, eleven school districts initiated FLES programs. Other districts formed committees and hired consultants to explore possibilities (Barnett, 1998, personal correspondence).

Why did these school districts decide to implement a FLES program? When asked this question, the responses from the thirteen districts with FLES programs fell into three categories, as shown in Table 1.

Table 1

Reasons for Implementing K-6 FLES Programs

Social or Global Awareness	Vision or Desire of Key Stakeholders	Educational or Competitive
➤ Increase in diversity of population of district ➤ World events ➤ Increase in importance of other languages for the community and the society at large	➤ Parents or PTA ➤ Superintendent ➤ Principal ➤ Foreign language Supervisor ➤ Foreign language Teacher	➤ Neighboring school districts have it ➤ Research showed this is the best time to begin a second language

The diversity issue is one that is likely to grow in the future years. In a series dedicated to Long Island's future, *Newsday*, highlighted the changes expected in the New York metropolitan area.

-A continued influx of ethic and racial minorities from as close as New York City and as far away as New Delhi, will surge…altering the personality of communities whose suburban identities have long been shaped by virtually all-white populations.

-Whites…who saw their majority remain firmly above 95 percent through the 1930s, '40s, '50s and '60s, will see an acceleration of the steep fall that began in the last two decades.

-By 2020…non-Hispanic whites will make up around six of 10 Long Islanders, down from eight of 10 today.

-The latest immigration figures covering 1990 to 1996 show that arrivals from El Salvador, the Dominican Republic, and India top the list of those identifying Long Island as their destination, followed by…Jamaica, Poland, and China.

-School officials in some districts have begun scrambling to develop policies to defuse what they fear will be escalating tensions between rival student cliques and parent groups (*Newsday*, January, 3, 1999, pp. H16-H29).

While a policy of foreign languages at the elementary schools may not be a panacea to the challenges of a diverse population, it is one attempt to foster understanding and facilitate communication in a substantive way; one that is built into the curriculum and daily experience for children.

The "vision" of the individuals who initiated FLES programs may overlap into other categories; yet, a consistency among them was the belief that this policy is "good for children." In many cases, it was a parent or board member who fought to have second languages as part of a child's program. For some school districts, looking at neighboring districts means keeping pace with an ideal and not missing out on something valuable.

Summary

The current status of a policy of early second language study is relatively positive. Countries around the world have a history of developing multilingual proficiencies through their educational systems. Nationally, several initiatives and guidelines call for early second language study (the National Standards, Educate America 2000, Educating America's Children for Tomorrow Act, The Education Excellence for All Children Act). On the state level, while the likelihood of a mandate for early introduction or an increased number of years of second language study is questionable, there is documentation of support for the policy.

Practice at the local level is more encouraging. Eleven school districts on Long Island implemented FLES programs in the last six years and four have implemented dual language immersion programs. The policies and practice of neighboring regions can impact on policy decisions in other areas. While policy may be informed by national and state-wide trends, locally developed policy is more aligned with the specific interests and needs of the local population. The interviews and analyses conducted in this document focus on the region of Long Island, New York, yet it is hoped that the data provided may inform school districts and policy makers across the nation.

Section Three

A Rationale for Early Second Language Study

What were the most salient rationales mentioned by educators for starting a FLES program? Global citizenry and enhanced language proficiency. Most school districts are interested in promoting harmonious relationships among diverse populations. Study of a second language can be tied to enhanced cross-cultural understanding and positive attitudes towards others (Carpenter & Torney, 1974). The importance of a long-term sequence of study in order to achieve proficiency in a second language is documented in research of foreign language and immersion programs (Corbin & Chiachere, 1997; Curtain, 1993; Genesee, 1983; Krashen, Scarcella, & Long, 1982; Long, 1990). This section will discuss the ideals of participation in global community, cross-cultural awareness, attitude enhancement, and enhanced proficiency in the second language.

Participation in a global community. Munks (1996) defended the notion that a multilingual citizen is open to new opportunities in the 21st century. The community, the government, and the private sector are areas where knowledge of a second language maximizes possibilities (p. 2).

> Interacting with our nation's increasingly diverse population requires a new kind of citizen-one who comes ready-made with skills in a language other than English…Before students born and educated in America can take advantage of these emerging opportunities the paradigm must be shifted (p. 3).

The paradigm shift from an English-only society, made of a melting pot of citizens, to a multilingual and pluralistic society is apparent in the statement of goals of elementary schools throughout the nation. Educators interviewed from several school districts mentioned mission statements or goals for learning including: acceptance and appreciation of others, developing a positive self-concept, enhanced communication skills, participating productively in our world, and expressing genuine concern for others. These goals cannot be realized without attending to the context of our communities.

Over sixty percent of the Long Islanders polled by *Newsday* stated that by 2020 they would expect to be attending schools in integrated communities. "Schools are already becoming anthropological laboratories, where the widening stream of ethnicities is providing children firsthand experience with lifestyles and values vastly different from their own " (*Newsday*, January, 3, 1999, p.7). Proficiency in a second language can assist children in developing the ability to participate in and understand the global community (Donato & Terry, 1995, Thompson et al., 1990; Tucker, 1990). Schools can assist children in using this knowledge of other cultures in a positive way.

Cross Cultural Awareness and Attitudinal Benefits. Cross-cultural understanding and acceptance are essential in a society that is as diverse as ours. "Learning is not and cannot be isolated from the needs of society" (Spinelli, 1996, p. 61). Since studies show that the age of ten is crucial to attitude development (Lambert & Klineberg, 1967) cross-cultural understanding and sensitivity is best developed in children under age ten (Rhodes et al., 1989; Riestra & Johnson, 1964).

> The purposes and uses of foreign languages are as diverse as the students who study them. Some students study another language in hopes of finding a rewarding career…Others are interested in the intellectual challenge…Still others seek greater understanding of other people and other cultures. It is with this philosophy in mind that the task force for the National Standards identified five

17

goal areas that encompass all of these reasons: Communication, Cultures, Connections, Comparisons, and Communities—the five C's of foreign language education (National Standards for Foreign Language Learning, 1996).

The National Standards for Foreign Language Learning focus on the knowledge and understanding of cultures, acquiring multiple ways of viewing the world, and enabling students to participate in multilingual communities. In order to attain these standards, students must develop positive attitudes towards other languages, peoples, and cultures. The goals of many FLES programs include the development of positive attitudes towards the language studied and towards people of other cultures (Curtain & Pesola, 1994; Lipton, 1998; Rhodes et al., 1989).

In a vision statement presented in the Annals of the American Academy of Political and Social Sciences, Brown (1994) stated,

> If foreign language learning is to be widely extended to the primary grades, the public must have a vision of what an American of the twenty-first century can and should be. A responsible and productive citizen will need to communicate with and understand people of different races and language groups. An early start in foreign language should provide the time to develop communication skills, the values necessary to live in a diverse society, and the ability to think critically (p. 173).

Starting Early for Enhanced Language Proficiency. Most school districts that implement K-5 FLES programs start implementation at Kindergarten. Their reasons include awareness of the research on "optimal age" and the belief that starting early means increased language proficiency. The most effective way to produce proficiency in a second language is to provide for long term study (Curtain, 1998; Curtain & Pesola, 1994, Dulay, Burt, & Krashen, 1982; Harley, 1998). "The language proficiency that students attain in any elementary school foreign language program is a direct result of the goals of the program and of the amount of time they spend in language study" (Curtain & Pesola, 1994, p. 256-7). Research on FLES programs indicates students who have experienced FLES have higher achievement in the second language later in life (American Council of Teachers of Foreign Languages, 1999; Brega & Newell, 1967; Donato, et al., 1996; Lipton, Morgan, & Reed, 1996; Mayuex et al., 1966; Vocolo, 1967; Vollmer, 1962).

Discussions related to the young child and foreign language learning often elicit observations and anecdotal accounts of how "younger is better," how young children learn another language more easily, and how they are superior in their learning of pronunciation. The general folklore around this belief is supported by research (Asher & Garcia, 1969; Dunkel & Pillet, 1957; Oyama, 1976; Yamada, et al., 1980) and publicity through media (Begley, 1996; Blakeslee, 1991, 1995; Nash, 1997) on the language processing ability of the brain and the experience of children in the classroom.

However, there exist empirical data that support the opposite conclusions, namely, that the older learner is more efficient at learning skills in the study a second language (Asher & Price, 1967; Fathman, 1975; Krashen, et al., 1979, 1982; Oller & Nagato, 1974; Olson & Samuels; 1973; Snow & Hoefnagel-Hohle, 1978). Most of these studies are short-term studies of young children versus adults, or they are difficult to generalize to other FLES models because they are based on ESL students. For example, Snow & Hoefnagel-Hohle's study (1978) included individuals who had moved to the region where the target language was spoken. These studies do not replicate the experience of a child in a FLES program. Long-term or studies of ultimate attainment in the second language tend to support a "sensitive period" for second language acquisition, indicating the importance of a long sequence of study (Krashen, et al., 1982; Long, 1990).

There is a wealth of research available on ESL and language-minority students. These studies are based on formal (school-setting) and naturalistic (acquisition through immersion in the culture of the language) experiences for children (Harley, 1986; Singleton & Lengyel, 1995). A widely held belief by scholars is that language-minority students should be educated in their native language early on and then receive instruction in the second language as their cognitive abilities improve. This is supported by many empirical and qualitative studies (Swain, 1981; Cummins, 1983b, 1984). However, the transfer of this theory and body of research onto the situation of the language-majority child learning a second language as an "elective" in a school setting is risky at best and confounding at worst. The experience of the language-minority child learning English as a second language is very different from a language-majority child learning a foreign language. The language-majority child already owns the dominant culture's language.

The optimal age theory began with the much-cited work of Penfield and Roberts (1959) and Lenneberg (1967). Penfield's theory was based on neurological studies of children and adults suffering from aphasia (temporary speech loss). He found when damage occurs to the left hemisphere of the brain (the area of speech), children are able to regain speaking abilities while adults may never regain this capacity. His explanation links a "plasticity" of the young brain with the ability to transfer speech to the other hemisphere. "After the age of ten or twelve, the general functional connections have been established and fixed in the speech cortex. After that, the speech center cannot be transferred to the cortex of the other side" (Penfield, 1964, p. 80). This plasticity also allows for the relative ease in the ability to acquire a second language if the child is exposed to the language during this formative period.

Lenneberg (1967) also argues for a "critical period hypothesis" in second language learning, claiming, for the older learner, "foreign languages have to be taught and learned through a conscious and labored effort" (p. 176). He specifically mentions the difficulty for the older child or adult to overcome foreign accents. The critique of these hypotheses from linguists is that they are based on pathological studies and so they may not necessarily be applicable to other experiences (Harley, 1986, Singleton, & Lengyel, 1995). Also, the critical period hypothesis does not explain the fluency gained by older individuals.

In July 1997, studies on healthy individuals at Memorial Sloan-Kettering Cancer Center in New York have found that "the capacity to speak a second language is stored in different places in the brain depending on when in life a person becomes bilingual" (New York Times, July 10, 1997). These studies, using Magnetic Resonance Imaging, have confirmed Penfield and Lenneberg's theories that language is stored in certain areas of the brain and is linked to certain biological stages. While this supports the critical period hypothesis, the cause of variation in acquisition for different ages still remains to be understood.

Krashen et al. (1979) reviewed research on age and attainment and found that the data on age, rate and attainment in second language acquisition are inconsistent. They generalize three findings from the literature on second language acquisition:

1. adults proceed through early stages of syntactic and morphological development faster that children (where time and exposure are held constant),

2. older children acquire faster than younger children (where time and exposure are held constant), and

3. acquirers who begin natural exposure to second languages during childhood generally achieve higher second language proficiency than those beginning as adults (p. 574).

These generalizations have become a "consensus view" among second language acquisition theorists (Singleton & Lengyel, 1995). "Short-term studies of instructed second language learning have indicated the same kind of initial advantage for older beginners as short-term studies of naturalistic L2 learning...The eventual benefits of early second language learning in a formal instructional environment might be expected to show up only in rather long-term studies than have to date been attempted" (p. 3). Long-term studies of early second language learning are needed to show the benefits of a longer sequence of learning.

Krashen (1979) restated the differences in learning for the age groups stating "older children in general initially acquire the second language faster than younger children (older is better for the rate of acquisition), but child second language acquirers will usually be superior in terms of ultimate attainment (younger is better in the long run)" (p. 574).

Summary

The interest in promoting harmonious relationships among diverse populations is increasing in our communities and schools. Since the study of a second language can be tied to enhanced cross-cultural understanding and positive attitudes towards others, a policy of FLES may provide this opportunity at an age that is optimal for attitude enhancement. This same age group may be able to acquire certain aspects of language proficiency better than older children. In addition, starting at a young age gives the learner the time necessary for improved overall language attainment. Swain (1981) discussed the importance of a longer sequence of instruction for second languages,

> For the majority child, the suggestion is that the second language be introduced as early as possible in a way that allows for the development of communicative skills. The reasons are threefold. First, the majority language child will need considerable opportunities to use the second language in natural communicative activities if he or she is to develop basic interpersonal skills in the second language. And, for the most part, the wider environment will not provide these opportunities. Second, the use of the first language in the wider environment ensures that it will not be lost through early second language learning...The third reason for the early introduction for the second language for majority language children rests in the factor of motivation. Adolescent learners may simply not perceive a need to put the time and energy into learning a second language (pp. 12-13).

Section Four

Argumentation for Implementing FLES Programs

This section of the document will present an argument for FLES programs.

Research on FLES programs is reviewed to support the ideals of cross-cultural

understanding and enhanced language proficiency. The goals of many FLES programs

include the development of positive attitudes towards the language studied and towards

people of other cultures (Curtain & Pesola, 1994; Lipton, 1998; Met, 1998; Rhodes et al.,

1989). The development of positive attitudes is both a means and an end in FLES

programs. These goals are reflected in the mission statements of many school districts

and in the National Standards for Foreign Languages (1996). Young children who study

a language are enjoying it, are interested in continuing the study, and feel positive about

the people of the target language. Even at risk and learning-disabled children may feel

success, sometimes for the first time, through the FLES experience.

Additional benefits related to the affective domain of the students are positive

self-concept and the desire to continue the study of the language and/or additional

languages (Donato et al., 1996; Hancock, et al., 1976; Masciantonio, 1977; Shrum, 1985).

These affective variables in second language learning are reciprocal in that the learner's

attitude towards the target language may enhance or inhibit second language learning

(Corbin & Chiachere, 1997; Schumann, 1975).

Argumentation for Cross-Cultural Awareness and Attitude Enhancement through FLES.

The study of affective development (attitude enhancement) is complex and challenging.

Implications of research in this area can be difficult to generalize because of the nature of

the construct. In spite of this, studies addressing attitude in second language learning provide findings that must be considered in the discussion of policy for foreign languages at the elementary school level. The conclusions that can be drawn from studies of the impact of FLES programs on attitude enhancement can be generalized as follows: (a) teaching a foreign language to elementary school children with a focus on the target culture is a potent force in creating more positive attitudes towards the peoples represented by that language (Riestra & Johnson, 1964; Rhodes et al., 1989), (b) children in a FLES program will be interested in continuing the study of a foreign language (Donato et al., 1996; Hancock, et al., 1976; Shrum, 1985), and (c) the study of a foreign language at the elementary school level appears to have a positive effect on the self-concept of all children (Masciantonio, 1977), including learning disabled and other at-risk children (Heining-Boynton, 1994; Shrum, 1985).

Before looking at the specific effects of a FLES program, it is important to understand what children's attitudes are in general towards people from other cultures, where the attitudes come from, and at what ages they formulate these attitudes. Lambert and Klineberg's study (1967) is pivotal as it addressed these areas in a multi-national study.

The sample for this study was 3,300 children at three age levels (6,10 and 14 years) from eleven different countries (U.S., South African Bantu, Brazil, English, Canada, French Canada, France, Germany, Israel, Japan, Lebanon, and Turkey). Yerxa (1970) highlighted the limitations of the study affecting its validity at points, namely: there were no African-American children in the sample from the United States, the children were all from one town in each region, teachers selected the children to be included in the study based on their assumptions about IQ and SES, and only urban children were selected (p. 26). In spite of these limitations, the study is noted for its expansiveness and the importance of the information regarding attitudes of children towards foreign cultures.

The purpose of the study was to examine the development of conceptions that children have of foreign peoples. The methods involved an open-ended interview which was structured enough to provide consistency, but flexible enough to allow for individual expressions to emerge (Lambert & Klineberg, 1967, p. 12). Children were asked to consider reactions they had to seven standard reference peoples (Americans, Brazilians, Chinese, Germans, Indians (from India), Africans, and Russians). Some of the questions (from a bank of 30) were, "What are you? What else are you? Are there people from other countries that are like you?....not like you? Do you like them? How do you know about them? In what way are they like/not like you?" (p. 231-37).

The responses were coded into five areas: responses of self-description, evaluative descriptions of others, content analysis of descriptions of standard reference peoples, affective evaluation of those "like us" and "not like us," and sources of information about other peoples. The data were presented as simple ratio scores. For example, the "index of similarity outlook" was determined by the number of foreign people categorized as similar over the total number of people thought of as either similar or dissimilar.

The study found six year-old children tended to believe most people were more different than similar to them. The 10 year olds' percentages for conceptions of similarities to the others were considerably higher. By age 10, the tendency to regard foreigners as similar reaches its maximum and does not change much between 10 and 14 years of age. With regard to affection for similars and dissimilars, again, six year-olds are consistently the least affectionate towards both. The 10 year-olds are the most friendly to dissimilars. The 10-year old age group was designated as the critical age for impressions of foreigners.

While parents were cited as the most important source of information at age six, the mass media, television, and movies were also cited. The media were the most common sources for the 10 and 14 year olds. One of the most important findings of this study is children who had friendly views of different foreigners also had more information about those people than the children who had unfriendly views (p. 175).

The researchers concluded self-conceptions of children greatly influence their views of others. At age six, children stress the differences between peoples and idealize their own groups. The child's first stereotype is of his or her own group. Comparable stereotypes of other nations do not appear until after age ten. This age group is the most receptive to foreigners. Whether these positive attitudes remain constant throughout the child's life will depend on "socio-cultural events which vary from group to group. These variations result from different, culturally-sanctioned methods of teaching children about foreign peoples" (Yerxa, 1970, p. 280).

There are three primary implications of the findings from this study for FLES program development. First, programs of foreign language study at the elementary school level with a strong cultural component provide an opportunity to enhance attitudes towards others at a time that is crucial for attitude development. Second, teachers of FLES programs should stress the similarities among cultures with children ages six or younger. Third, FLES teachers should capitalize on the openness of 10 year-olds for enhancement of the understanding of and interest in other peoples, cultures, and languages. These practices support the fourth of the National Standards for Foreign Language Learning (1996), "understanding the concept of culture through comparisons of cultures studied and one's own" (p. 9).

Two studies reviewed (Rhodes et al., 1989; Riestra & Johnson, 1964) have findings that support the theory of FLES as a means for greater understanding and acceptance of peoples from other cultures. Three years prior to the Lambert and Klineberg study, Riestra and Johnson (1964) conducted a similar study on attitudes of children towards foreign-speaking peoples. Their study focused on testing the theory that children in FLES programs (experimental group) have better attitudes towards foreign people than students who are not exposed to FLES (control group). FLES students learning Spanish consistently selected more positive attitudes to describe people from Spanish-speaking countries than the non-FLES students.

In the Rhodes et al. study (1989), student attitudes towards other languages and cultures were examined through an attitude survey ("What do YOU think?"). The survey was designed specifically for this study and was based on the attitude survey of Gardner and Smythe (1974). It included questions regarding feelings towards native speakers, interest in the foreign language, parental encouragement and attitudes towards classroom experience.

The findings showed positive attitudes for students in all programs (FLEX, FLES, and immersion) towards the target language and culture. The benefits of attitude development in even the least intensive program model (FLEX) are noteworthy. The authors concluded that the results on the survey were encouraging.

Hancock, Lipton, and Baslow (1976) specifically looked at the effects of FLES on attitudes towards the study of a foreign language. The sample was 261 sixth grade students. The researchers used an attitude scale developed for the study. In surveying both FLES and non-FLES students, they assessed the importance each group placed on learning a second language. One of the questions asked the students if they thought understanding other cultures could, in part, resolve world problems. Sixty-two percent of the FLES students felt this was true, while 33% of the non-FLES students responded positively. Fifty percent of the FLES students agreed with the necessity to learn a foreign language and 22% of the non-FLES students agreed with this statement.

When asked if foreign languages were important for them, 80% of the FLES and non-FLES students combined thought they were. While only half of the FLES students expressed the need to learn a foreign language, most children, both FLES and non-FLES had positive attitudes towards the importance of learning a foreign language. The implications of this study are children believe studying a foreign language is a valuable and important experience.

Donato, Antonek & Tucker (1994, 1995, 1996) have conducted an on-going program evaluation of a Japanese FLES program. One of the components of the study is a "Language and Culture Questionnaire" (based on the attitude survey of Gardner & Smythe, 1981). The purposes of the attitude survey were to obtain information on student attitudes towards the study of Japanese in particular, motivation to continue with the language study, and perceptions of parental encouragement for studying the language. The 1995 and 1996 studies showed a strong majority of the FLES students in grades K-5 were enjoying the study of the language (74% and 85% respectively). The 1994 data presented statistical analyses, which also showed a positive result. The desire to continue studying the language was positive for 73% of the students in the 1996 study. In the 1995 study, 58% of the K-2 group and 47% of grades 3 - 5 wanted to continue study of the language. The 1994 statistics showed the same positive results.

The authors further analyzed the results by examining the relationship of these attitudes to other measures. In the 1994 study, the effects of parental encouragement on performance on the language achievement test had the strongest relationship. The 1996 study examined age as a factor in attitude development. The younger group (K-2) consistently held more positive attitudes towards the program than the older group. The authors conclude,

> This finding does not suggest that the older cohort disliked learning a new language since 49% of the older children were found to be consistently positive about learning Japanese, whereas only 18% systematically reported negative reactions. What this finding does indicate, however, is that age, rather than gender is related to attitudinal responses (p. 17).

These findings are not directly related to the Lambert and Klineberg findings (1967) since they are specific to a FLES program, and they do not discuss attitudes towards foreign peoples. However, it would be interesting to continue the analysis of the effect age has on attitudes developed towards other peoples through a FLES program. The Donato et al. studies are unique in that they are the only FLES studies that address the effect of age on attitude development (i.e. the younger FLES student as opposed to the older). In addition to the age factor, the understanding of attitude development towards speakers of the target language and other languages and cultures (not just attitudes towards the study of the language) for FLES programs must be researched further.

Several studies discussed the effects of a FLES program on the self-concept of learning-disabled children. A qualitative paradigm was used to assess attitudes in Shrum's study (1985) of a small rural school district in southwestern Virginia. As part of an evaluation of a FLES program for fifth and sixth graders, Shrum conducted ethnographic interviews to examine attitudes towards studying the language as well as overall impressions and effects of the program. Fifteen interviews with seventeen open-ended questions were conducted with students, teachers, parents and administrators. Findings from the interviews indicated, "The most distinguishing feature of the program is the enthusiasm it generates for learning among students" (p. 9). The children are thoroughly enjoying the language learning experience; they are "learning…without a struggle" and are "real excited about the class" (p. 9).

Shrum stated the most exciting effect of the program is the improved attitude and academic performance of the learning disabled and other at-risk children in the group. She provided samples of respondents' comments regarding these children:

-One child was the worst child in everything; now this child is the best in

French and good in everything.

-A label has been removed from a retarded child since he now sits in 5th

grade [language] classroom.

-A slow reader who compensates by listening has a boosted self-image.

-In this program the LD child has more advantages than the gifted child.

-Average and below-average students are excited to find that they can compete with kids that have been showing them up all these years in

reading and writing (p. 10).

An advocate for early language learning and an experienced teacher of the learning

disabled child, Barnett (1986) stated,

> The inclusion of students of all abilities [is] the main reason for [the FLES]
>
> program having survived a period of decline [experienced in other districts].
>
> Satisfied students make satisfied parents who will not allow school boards or
>
> administrators to delete those very subjects which keep them most satisfied.
>
> Many times, the foreign language classroom, which was teaching to many
>
> learning modalities, was the one in which the students felt the greatest measure of
>
> success (p. 5).

FLES programs may also have a positive impact on the self-concept of children

who are not learning disabled. Masciantonio (1977) discusses research from FLES

programs for Latin in California and Massachusetts. The California project was effective

in "improving student knowledge of word origin…structural analysis, [and] increasing

the self-concept and interest in language study of students" (p. 380). In the

Massachusetts program, the researchers found an "improvement in self-image,

motivation, and self-reliance in the pilot group" (p. 381). While these positive outcomes

may not be stated as specific goals for a FLES program, future research may continue to

examine the effect of FLES programs on self-concept as it is a construct that is gaining

more importance in our educational systems.

In summary, the studies reviewed here of the effects of FLES programs on the

development of positive attitudes towards the language, towards others, and self-concept are encouraging. More studies of FLES programs with specific attention to attitudes towards others are needed.

Argumentation for Enhanced Language Proficiency through FLES. The scarcity of studies of the effects of age in FLES programs for language-majority students is reflected in this section of the analysis of the policy (a total of six were found after extensive searching; one was dated 1996, the others were from the 1950s to the 1970s). This reflects the need for future research in this area. FLES programs currently in existence should be studied for the effects of age on the development of language skills, and in order to have the greatest benefit to informing our practices in schools, they should be longitudinal studies.

The studies reviewed below provide evidence that the younger child in a FLES program is more successful in the skills of listening, phonology, and speaking than the older child. The age range for comparisons in the studies reviewed were Kindergarten, first, third, fourth, and fifth grade compared with performance against third, seventh, eighth, ninth, tenth and eleventh grade students.

Of the earlier studies (Brega & Newell, 1967; Mayuex & Dunlap, 1966; Vocolo, 1967; Vollmer, 1962), only Brega and Newell and Vocolo included assessment of all four skills, speaking, listening, reading and writing. They both found that students who studied languages at the elementary level out-performed peers who had studied only briefly at the secondary level in all areas of the assessments used. (In the Vocolo study the FLES and the non-FLES students had equal performance in reading skills.) The Mayuex & Dunlap study (1966) showed superiority in listening skills for the FLES students over the non-FLES students and the Vollmer study showed a 10% gain in grades

33

on report cards for high school students who had FLES. The implication is beginning foreign language study at a younger age is preferable because it increases the time that students are studying the language, and may allow for increased proficiency in the language.

The Lipton, Morgan & Reed (1996) survey found French AP students who had FLES in grades one-three scored higher on the AP examination. The years of study correlated with the scores as shown in Table 2.

Table 2

Results for FLES Students on AP French (Lipton, Morgan, Reed, 1996)

Grade Started	Average AP Grade (highest score=5, lowest score=1)
1-3	3.25
4-6	2.95
7-9	2.84
10-12	2.32

The younger the starting age is the higher the ultimate attainment on the AP exam.

The most recent long-term study of the effect of age in second language learning (Donato, Antonek & Tucker, 1996), examined age differences and language proficiency for FLES students of Japanese in the Falk School (a laboratory school of the University of Pittsburgh). Thirty-one students were divided into two groups—K-2 students (16) and students in grades 3-5 (15). Students were matched for ability using scores on the California Achievement Test.

The PRO-I (Prochievement Interview) and the SOF (Scores for Observer and Teacher) were used to assess both oral proficiency in meaningful and realistic context, as well as comprehension, fluency, grammar, pronunciation and vocabulary. A moderate, yet significant, correlation was found for age group and performance in favor of the older student on the PRO-I test. The SOF scores also indicated an advantage for older children. The one exception was in pronunciation. The younger students outperformed the older students in this area.

An analysis of variability among mean scores for each group showed the older group exhibited a wider range of abilities. The authors conclude, "Although some of the older children outperformed younger children, an early start may result in more uniform gains for the majority of learners in the long term. In other words, beginning language instruction in the early primary years may result in greater success for a greater number of students" (p. 372). This study confirms the belief that a longer sequence of language study, beginning at the early primary levels, will improve linguistic performance.

In the third year of the study, 1996, the authors provided a careful examination of the effect of age by using a growth curve analysis. The results of this analysis of vocabulary knowledge and language production showed differences in rates of attainment for different children. When looking specifically at age, they conclude, "in addition to the more positive attitudes towards language learning…the younger learners perform as well, if not occasionally better than, older children in elementary school" (p. 28) on the language skills examined.

In summary, while the "sensitive age" for beginning second language study is not proven beyond doubt, certain aspects of second language development may be dependent upon the starting age. In a review of the research on the effect of age on second language learning, Long (1990) stated,

> The ability to attain native-like phonological abilities in a second language begins
> to decline by age 6 in many individuals and to be beyond anyone beginning later

than age 12…Native-like morphology and syntax only seem to be possible for

those beginning before age 15 (p. 280).

The studies reviewed in this section indicate that as the length of study increases, there is

also a positive effect on performance in the language at later stages.

<u>Summary</u>

This argumentation for a FLES policy to develop cross-cultural understanding and

improve language proficiency may be summarized around five main points: (a) exposing

children under ten to second language study may foster positive attitudes towards people

of other languages and cultures, (b) attitudes towards learning a second language may be

enhanced by starting in the early elementary grades, (c) FLES may have a positive effect

on the self-concept of all children, (d) the younger learner may have an advantage in

listening and pronunciation skills, and (e) a FLES program may improve performance in

the second language in later years. The degree of success in these areas is contingent

upon the characteristics and goals of the program offered such as the amount of time

provided, the length of exposure, the instructional methodology, and the vertical and

horizontal articulation of the program.

Section Five

The Ideal FLES Model

The purpose of this document is to provide policymakers with a model of early language instruction that is accessible for most school districts. This model is based on information from primary research, related literature, interviews with leaders in the field, and interviews with people who are currently involved in implementing this type of program.

The Ideal Model proposed has 18 components. This model is based on the arguments for adopting a FLES model provided in Section Four. The description of the Ideal Model is presented in Table 3. It is followed by a discussion and argumentation for each of the 18 components in Section Six.

The 18 components should be seen as guidelines for a successful FLES program based on the experience of many educators. While some aspects of the components might not seem feasible for all districts, they can be viewed as an "ideal" or target. Decisions made based on the needs and interests of each school district might fall short of these ideals. It is important to note that everyone interviewed for this document felt it was best to strive for the most comprehensive, the most rewarding, the ideal; and then deal with necessary compromises from that perspective.

At the time of the writing of this document, two school districts were considering partial immersion programs. Most immersion programs on Long Island exist in communities with a large population of non-English speakers. The two districts were examining the immersion model for its strength in outcomes of language learning and development of a multicultural attitude. As stated above, a strong sequential FLES model may serve the needs of many districts. Yet immersion is considered the most powerful model for early language learning.

The FLES model is a "gateway" program for districts to consider. It is a model that any district should be able to implement. A partial immersion model could be implemented with children enrolling on a "voluntary" basis. That would allow for maintaining a "school within a school." The main difference in terms of staffing is that the immersion program requires hiring (or replacing current staff with) bilingual teachers.

Table 3

The 18 Components of an "Ideal FLES Model"

Participation of classroom teachers, foreign language teachers from all levels, administrators, and parents through a FLES committee
Goals reflecting language proficiency, cultural proficiency, and content from the elementary curriculum
Instruction five times a week
Scheduling: Kindergarten and First grade—15-20 minutes per session,   Second and Third grade—20-30 minutes per session,   Fourth and Fifth grade—30-40 minutes per session,   Sixth grade—40 minutes per session
Inclusion of ALL students
Content-related instruction (themes from the elementary curriculum)
Mutual planning time for FLES teachers and classroom teachers
Multifaceted curriculum (including teacher-prepared materials, other materials reflecting the goals of the program, and technology)
Strong cultural component
Instruction presented in the target language
Staff certified in FLES methodology
Staff development and networking opportunities
Language choice based on district's needs/interests
Multiple entry points to study other languages (sixth grade, ninth grade)
Plans for articulation with the middle school and high school
Multiple assessment techniques (authentic assessment, achievement tests)
Program evaluation
Community support and public relations

Section Six

Argumentation and Discussion of the 18 Components

This section will discuss the 18 components of the Ideal FLES model and will

provide an argument for each component. Some of the components are grouped together

as they are related to one another in the discussion presented.

- **Participation of classroom teachers, foreign language teachers from all levels,**
  administrators, and parents through a FLES committee

One of the first steps in the process is to establish a committee. The committee

should include administration, second language teachers (from the elementary and

secondary levels), elementary classroom teachers, union representatives, parents, and

community members. The planning process that includes representation form all

interested parties is the most likely to succeed (Curtain & Pesola, 1994). The majority of

the school districts that have implemented FLES programs report a minimum of one year

from formation of the committee to implementation of the program.

The first task of the committee is to investigate current FLES programs and to

review literature and research on FLES. Through the research available, the committee

should be able to support the rationale for a FLES program. The research will also bring

to light obstacles and options. As discussion around the policy continues, goals must be

written, based on the rationale for the program (development of cultural awareness, a

degree of language proficiency, learning language through content).

Who initiates the idea for implementation of the policy or forms the committee?

The initiation may come from several sources. Table 4 shows the six sources of initiation

for successfully implemented (K-6) FLES programs.

Table 4

Examples of Individuals Who Initiated the Idea of a FLES Program

Initiator	Number of Schools
Foreign Language Teacher	4
Community member	3
Principal	2
PTA	2
Superintendent	2
Foreign Language Chairperson	1

The committee should conduct visitations of other programs to inform themselves about successful programs. A list of questions related to implementation may help the FLES committee reflect on important issues as they determine how to best implement a FLES program. These questions may also be helpful during visitations to school districts with FLES programs (see Table 5). Several districts hire consultants to expedite the gathering of data, answer important questions that arose, and provide relevant information. Data gathered from the research and literature on these issues will guide the FLES committee along with the information collected from visitations. The FLES committee should meet regularly to discuss issues and to write a proposal for the district.

Table 5

FLES Committee and Visitation Questions

Who will be on the committee?
How often will we meet?
How will we handle disagreements?
What are the goals of the program?
How will we fit this into the school day?
How will it be scheduled?
In which grade(s) will it start?
Which language(s) will be offered?
How will we staff the program?
How much will it cost?
From where will we get the money?
How do we incorporate content from the elementary curriculum?
How will culture be incorporated?
Which materials will we purchase?
Who will write the curriculum?
How does technology fit into this plan?
How do we ensure articulation with the middle school and high school?
How will we assess the progress of the students?
How will we evaluate the program?
How do we attend to the needs of ALL students?
Should we make special provisions for the less-able learner?
How do we ensure the program is offering equal access to knowledge for all students?
How should we inform the public about the implementation process, including the successes and failings of the program?

A single individual cannot adequately address these issues with all the complexities and many implications they present. The process of implementation is made easier through the efforts of all individuals on the committee.

- **Goals reflecting language proficiency, cultural proficiency, and content from the elementary curriculum**

One of the first tasks for the committee is to develop goals for the program. The goals established will effect decisions regarding many aspects of the program (i.e.

language proficiency, reinforcement of elementary curriculum, etc.). In addition to supporting the National Standards (Communication, Culture, Comparisons, Connections, Community), the goals of the program should reflect the mission of the school or school district (Curtain & Pesola, 1994). For example, the mission statement of a school district on Long Island states, "[The school district], a Community of Learners, through its educational programs, promotes intellectual curiosity and creative expression, values diversity, and measures success by one's personal development and contribution to society." If this district were to consider a policy of early second language study, its goals should incorporate these concepts.

Table 6 shows the mutual support of concepts in a comparison of the goals of the total elementary program of a school district with the goals of a FLES program.

Table 6

Comparison of Elementary Goals with FLES Goals

Goals of a 2nd Grade Program:	Goals of a FLES Program:
To be a caring, thinking, productive Participant in our world	To acquire an understanding of and appreciation for other cultures
Function healthfully, socially, and economically	To acquire proficiency in listening and speaking (with some proficiency in reading and writing) in the target language
Skills in literacy, math, science, technology, social sciences, and the arts are best developed incrementally, beginning at the appropriate stages in the child's academic career	To use the content areas of the elementary curriculum to engage students in acquiring skills in the target language

- **Instruction five times a week**

- **Scheduling: Kindergarten and First grade—15-20 minutes per session,
                 Second and Third grade—20-30 minutes per session,
                 Fourth and Fifth grade—30-40 minutes per session,
                 Sixth grade—40 minutes per session**

These two components relate to the scheduling design of the model and the impact on expected outcomes. Arguments for this amount of instruction are based on effectiveness of the FLES model in relation to the other options (FLEX or Immersion). The immersion models are the most effective in developing language proficiency (Rhodes et al., 1989). The FLEX model is able to provide students with an exposure to basic words and phrases and cultural awareness (Curtain & Pesola, 1994). The (Sequential) FLES model offers a continuous program with the goal of language proficiency and cultural awareness while also being able to reinforce the elementary curriculum through content-related instruction (Orringer, 1998). It is a combination of the goals of the other two models with less commitment required on the part of the school district than for an immersion model and with more language proficiency expected than with the FLEX model.

Most school districts implementing early second language programs tend to select the FLES model. Why do these districts choose FLES over FLEX or immersion? The people interviewed for this analysis opted for the FLES model for several reasons. At least four of the school districts used research as the guide for the best model for their district characteristics and goals. Those four districts along with five others visited other successful programs throughout Long Island and New York State in order to learn from them. Through the visitations, they determined FLES was the best model. Many districts chose the model because it provided the most language with the least disruption to the school day (for an in depth discussion of model choice, see Section Eight).

It is important to note that while FLES models may vary in the amount of time allowed for instruction, a minimum of 75 minutes per week has been recommended by leaders in the field of second language study (Rosenbusch, 1992). Curtain and Pesola (1994) clarified the fact that "the level of language fluency a student will gain in an elementary school foreign language class is directly related to the amount of time students spend learning the language, and on the intensity of that language experience (p. 256)." In the Performance Guidelines for K-12 learners, the American Council of Teachers of Foreign Languages gives a visual representation of the anticipated outcomes based on length and age at the start of second language study which shows the greatest advantage for the long sequence of study (see Appendix F).

- **Inclusion of ALL students**

The ideal FLES program is made available to all students, including special education students, at risk students, and learning disabled students. Special education students and children of diverse learning abilities can also enjoy the many personal and intellectual benefits of early second language study (Baker, 1995; Barnett, 1986; Bruck, 1987). If a learning-disabled child is struggling to master aspects of his or her native language, the metalinguistic knowledge gained by studying a second language may aid in this process (Anadrade et al., 1989, p. 192). Studies of students in immersion programs indicate learning-disabled children perform as well as above-average students on oral production and interpersonal communication tasks (Genesee, 1976a, 1976b, 1983). At the elementary school level, learning a second language is less dependent on previous verbal learning than most other areas of the curriculum (Curtain & Pesola, 1994, p. 9), so the "playing field is more level."

Barnett (1999) discussed techniques for working with the learning-disabled student such as "scaffolding" (providing students with visual aids to support learning of words) as well as the use of alternative assessments. In an interview about learning-disabled (LD) foreign language students, she explained,

> The expectations of success [should not be lowered] when it comes to the LD student—they can succeed as well as in other classes…sometimes even better. The "communicative mode" in the Standards is so closely attuned to their way of learning. In fact, I commend the Standards for what has been the greatest change in attitude towards LD students because they were designed for ALL students—specifically stating that ALL students can be successful as language and culture learners (p. 6).

The conceptual framework underlying the method of instruction may also have implications for the less-able learner. Through the communicative approach, natural, "hands-on" experiences may create a positive learning environment for children with certain learning styles. The philosophy of instruction for a FLES classroom does not include an emphasis on studying grammatical forms. The focus on the development of oral/aural skills through experiential learning may allow for greater success and feelings of competence for these students.

The teacher's belief system for the abilities of these students is another key to their success. A teacher who does not believe ALL students can learn may have difficulty fostering a positive self-concept in the learning-disabled child.

In today's society, educators should take advantage of all opportunities to enhance the self-concept of students. Shrum (1985) stated the most exciting effect of a FLES program is the improved attitude and academic performance of the learning-disabled children (p. 10). Evidence from research on FLES programs in California and

Massachusetts indicates improvement in the self-concept, self-image, motivation, and self-reliance of children studying Latin (Masciantonio, 1977).

Many FLES teachers interviewed for this document explained that all learning disabled children included in the program were experiencing great success. In some cases, separate FLES classes were arranged for special education students. All of the teachers interviewed expressed the belief that these students can learn (and enjoy) a second language. Some schools use the FLES class time to give students resource time or instruction in ESL. For the most part, ESL students were included in the FLES class. Teachers felt this was "their opportunity to shine" especially if the target language was their native language. For students whose native language was different, the expression "leveling the playing field" was used to describe their experience. For example, Asian students who were in Spanish FLES classes, while learning English, were as engaged and successful as other students.

For many years people believed a study of a second language should be offered to the "gifted" or "above average" student (Anadrade et. al, 1989; Spinelli, 1996). Two studies of FLES programs (Adcock, 1980; Garfinkel & Tabor, 1991) indicated the slightly "below average" or "average" student also gains in achievement on assessment of vocabulary skills and reading scores through participation in a FLES program.

There is a growing body of research on the less-able learner and techniques for instruction to allow for success in the second language (Sparks, et. al, 1991; Sparks & Ganschow, 1993). The essence of these studies is that a multi-sensory approach to instruction would allow the less-able learner to be successful. These studies are based on the high school and college student. It is possible that the less-able learner who is offered second language in the early primary grades may not have as much difficulty with learning the language later on in school. Future research may examine this possibility.

Several FLES teachers interviewed stressed the successful experiences of the less-able learners in their classes:

-If they hadn't told me that this student has learning problems, I would not have thought so. I see her doing just as well as the others. I almost wish I didn't know that.

-I have a boy who has severe Down 's syndrome. He is so enthusiastic in the FLES class. He was the first of all my students, all of them, to learn the words to a song about months. He is just thriving in the class.

-One of my students was told he would not be coming to class so that he could go to resource room. He became very upset, he started to cry. He insisted on coming to class. He did not want to miss it. It is an opportunity for him to be successful right along side of the others.

- **Content-related instruction**

   (incorporating themes from the elementary curriculum)

- **Mutual planning time for FLES teachers and classroom teachers**

   The approach to instruction in a FLES program should be focused on language development, while at the same time including content from the elementary curriculum. In content-based (or content-related) classrooms, the language is used as a medium to present the content of the elementary curriculum.

Curtain and Pesola (1994) further distinguished between content-based and content-related instruction. Content-based instruction is similar to immersion, with the foreign language teacher being responsible for teaching and assessing certain elements of the curriculum. Content-related instruction allows the foreign language teacher to "borrow" themes and concepts from the elementary curriculum to weave into the language class. In a content-based program, the FLES teacher follows the time schedule for instruction of certain concepts, as they are planned throughout the year for each grade level. In a content-related program, the FLES teacher uses themes from the curriculum after they have already been presented to the classes. The FLES teacher may even present the concepts a year or two after the original presentation by the classroom teacher. It is revisited, reviewed, and re-taught in a new way, using the target language.

What is the purpose of tying the instruction of the language to the curriculum? First, as noted in several of the studies cited throughout this document, the method of instruction may have an impact on the success and effect of the program. Second, language theorists discuss the importance of meaningful, cognitively engaging, and contextualized language learning experiences (Cummins, 1981; Krashen, 1981; Omaggio-Hadley, 1992). The greater these aspects of the instructional experience, the greater the retention and acquisition of the second language. Haas (1999) presented case studies of three FLES teachers using content-related instruction and noted the successful outcomes for students in language, content, and culture.

In order for instruction to be meaningful, engaging and contextualized, the FLES teacher may borrow content and instructional techniques from the classroom teacher, while allowing the children to use the second language.

Use of the target language to teach general curriculum content in this way enhances the effectiveness of language instruction in two ways. First, it increases the actual amount of time the learner spends in meaningful use of the target language, thus increasing the rate and amount of language learning that can take place. Second, students who are actively engaged with learning important information, using the new language as a tool, are experiencing the target language in a way that makes it both more meaningful and more memorable (Pesola, 1995, p.36).

Leaders in the field of second language instruction claim children are given another opportunity to learn the content, perhaps in a way they will be able to understand, relate to, and retain (Barnett, 1999, personal communication). Research on immersion and second language acquisition also supports the theory that children are able to gain proficiency in content and language simultaneously (Dulay, Burt, & Krashen, 1982; Genesee, 1987).

FLES teachers describe successes in applying content-related instruction:

-It is so wonderful to see all the lights go on and excitement in their eyes when I am reading a story that they just read in class, but now it's in Spanish.

-I thought it would be a lot more difficult. Working with the classroom teacher has made it so much more possible for me.

-Using the elementary curriculum has made my job easier, actually. I enjoy it more.

-I wish I could do it more often. I don't have enough time to prepare what would be necessary. I also don't get to meet with the teacher enough.

Some school districts with FLES programs have established content-related instruction as the approach for their FLES model. This approach also generates support for a FLES program as it reduces the time taken away from other subject areas, by providing for a review of the elementary curriculum. Content-related instruction follows philosophically with the trend in elementary education for holistic and integrated learning (Pesola, 1995, p.12).

Applying content-related instruction is more than just presenting the content. It is also the application of instructional techniques of the elementary classroom. These techniques include graphic organizers, charts, webbing, flow charts, storybook writing, Venn diagrams, etc. (Curtain & Pesola, 1994). The content-related classroom must maintain a focus on meaningful use of language while presenting material. Children must be given the opportunity to interact while working with the content. For example, in a second grade class, the FLES teacher may be reinforcing the scientific concepts in the metamorphosis of the caterpillar into a butterfly. During one of the FLES lessons using this content, children could pretend to be the caterpillar and the butterfly and ask each other questions, such as, "Who are you? Where did you come from?" (Sample content-related FLES lessons are presented in Appendix N.) Examining materials for immersion classes provides a key into the possibilities for coordinating with content areas (Lorenz & Met, 1990).

In 1998, the New York State Education Department published the *Early Elementary Resource Guide to Integrated Learning*. In this guide, the standards for each content area are supported through activities that integrate the learning experience across content areas. Teachers throughout New York State write the examples for activities in the guide. Each activity is constructed around a learning concept. Through this concept,

each of the five content areas are integrated in a meaningful way (English language arts,

the arts, career development/occupational, mathematics/science/technology, studies, and

languages other than English). Table 7 provides an example from the guide (p. 26).

Table 7

Example of an Integrated Learning Chart for Elementary Curricula

Learning Concept: BANKING
English Language Arts: • Listen to stories and discussion, share ideas, read notes, write messages, follow instructions, ask questions • discuss vocabulary and concepts related to banking • pose questions and seek answers regarding the functions of various types of banks
Mathematics, Science, and Technology: • create a realistic banking environment • apply basic number concepts in observation of banking operations and role playing
The Arts: • create classroom props using a variety of materials and tools
Career Development and Occupational Studies: • compare banking to other jobs • describe the kinds of work people do in specific settings, and the skills and tools they need to perform their jobs
Languages Other Than English: • examine the monetary units of the target language countries • role play exchanging American currency to that of a target language country

Crandall and Tucker (1990) described the eight areas that must be addressed for

successful implementation of content-related programs. These areas are: deriving

instructional objectives, developing background knowledge, content-compatible

language, social language, materials, multiple media, hands-on learning experiences, and

writing. The authors explained that the critical factor in successfully addressing these

issues is the support of an administrator "who provides for planning, pre-service, and in-

service training and curriculum development" (p. 196).

Curtain and Haas (1995) also gave guidelines for integrating curriculum in a FLES program. They explained that the FLES teacher should,

1. Become familiar with the regular classroom curriculum by observing… students' regular classes.

2. Plan to integrate content that you are interested in…start on a small scale.

3. Use a web or curriculum planning format that promotes the integration of language, content, and culture.

4. Design interesting activities for the students that…use prior knowledge, ask students to work in a variety of groupings…use holistic strategies…challenge the students to think critically…address multiple ways of learning (p. 4).

While content-related instruction provides advantages for the program and for the second language learner, it also presents challenges and difficulties. Genesee (1991) explained that effective second language instruction does not lose sight of the importance of meaningful interaction. The program must balance three concepts, (1) integrating language and content, (2) encouraging extensive interaction among classmates, and (3) include a systematic focus on language development. A comprehensive look at these issues is discussed by Snow, Met, and Genesee (1989) who stressed the importance of focusing on meaningful use of language while engaging students in interaction with the content.

Another issue that arises is the concern over what is to be corrected if there is an error produced by the child during interaction of the student with the content; the language or the content? A leader in second language instruction at the elementary level responded to this question, "You correct both."

In a content-related classroom, the FLES teacher must feel able to present the material. Cloud (1998) discussed the complexities of this situation, "While language teachers are being urged more and more to engage in content-based language teaching using this approach, the reality is that they usually do their teaching in isolation, without an active working knowledge of the subject matter and with limited collaboration with subject matter specialists (p. 116)."

Several school districts have established staff development programs with the intention of assisting in this area. In addition, if the classroom teacher is expected to remain in the classroom during the FLES session (i.e. s/he is not given a prep period for this time), the collaboration between the two teachers is more likely. Through collaboration, content-related instruction is more likely to be a success. One of the districts provided for intensive collaboration through curriculum writing and meeting sessions during the summer for the classroom teacher with the FLES teacher. A bibliography of content-based materials and literature prepared by Audrey Heining-Boynton is presented in Appendix I.

- **Multifaceted curriculum (including teacher-prepared materials, other materials reflecting the goals of the program, and technology)**

   Appropriate and engaging instructional materials for a FLES program may be found in educational catalogues or in the homes of the students and teachers in the program. Many content-related materials may already be available through sharing with the classroom teacher (such as manipulatives, realia, models, picture books, etc.). "In all types of elementary school foreign language programs, if materials are to be developed or adapted locally, time and adequate funding for their preparation must be included in the implementation plan" (Rosenbusch, 1991, p. 304).

While adequate funding will give support to a comprehensive model, in many programs, teachers are using simple items (puppets made from socks, stuffed animals, empty boxes turned into magic boxes) to bring excitement and learning together for children.

When asked about materials used in the FLES programs, most teachers responded with similar experiences.

-I make a lot of my materials. I find it more time consuming, but

better in the long run because I know these things will work for my kids.

-I enjoy experimenting with different things. I think we have a decent budget for

our program. I love using big books, for example, and they can be expensive, but

when I can't find a book I would like to use, I just cover over the English words

in one of the books from the classroom teacher.

-I guess I wish I had a bigger budget, but there isn't a whole lot out there that

really fits the bill, as far as I'm concerned. I think there's more and more coming

out now.

The same type of discussion was shared regarding the development of curriculum. Many FLES teachers develop their own curriculum. In the content-related programs, some teachers worked with classroom teachers to align the curriculum in a seamless model. In some districts, curriculum materials were sought from abroad to provide students with content-based and language specific resources. Two concerns arose with this practice. First, it can become very costly. Second, the material may not always be age-appropriate given the limited level of language proficiency of the students. Care must be taken to use material that is culturally appropriate, cognitively engaging, practical in use, and language-focused.

There are commercially prepared packages designed for bilingual programs in the United States that may provide supplementary materials for a content-related FLES program. The National K-12 Foreign Language Resource Center has publications geared towards thematic instruction (see Appendices I and M). Countless references for content-related materials can be found on websites for early second language instruction (see Appendix M).

Most programs expect to continue the development of curriculum throughout the beginning years of the program. Meeting with classroom teachers on a regular basis, exploring available materials, experimenting with technology, and maintaining a focus on the importance of culture, content, and language, will allow FLES teachers to make informed decisions about curriculum and materials.

The *Framework for FLES Curriculum* prepared by Pesola (1995) is a comprehensive plan for developing curriculum for early second language learning. Its purpose is to aid teachers since most FLES curricula are self-prepared. Pesola explained,

> There is an urgent need for a guiding framework for curriculum development for elementary school foreign language programs that takes in to account all of the contemporary influences on curriculum at the elementary school level. Because FLES programs are the most numerous, have the longest tradition in this country, and have the greatest potential for bringing significant language learning

opportunities to large numbers of students, a curriculum framework for FLES

programs seems to warrant the highest priority (p. 5).

An administrator of a FLES program echoed Pesola's explanation of the difficulties in

curriculum preparation for some teachers.

> -The FLES teachers in the program were not trained in elementary level
>
> child development and curriculum. Even if we did have an elementary teacher
>
> writing the curriculum though, she would probably not be familiar with the new
>
> standards or other second language issues.

FLES educators around the country piloted Pesola's curriculum framework. The

responses to its usefulness were overwhelmingly high. In spite of the concern that it was

time consuming, teachers felt "the extra time was worth it" (p. 101).

Process for Curriculum Development

1. Identify sources of outcomes

    a. Lists of language functions

    b. Inventory of cultural symbols, products, practices (or Culture Scope and

       Sequence)

    c. Lists of outcomes for the content areas of the curriculum

2. Choose a thematic center

3. Brainstorm potential content for the theme, with special emphasis on potential for

   story form and story telling

4. Choose outcomes for the theme

    a. language in use outcomes

    b. culture outcomes

c. subject content outcomes

5. Address the next level of decisions

    a. assessment

    b. activities

    c. grammatical structures

    d. vocabulary

       -receptive

       -expressive

    e. materials

    f. classroom setting

6. Define student outcomes

From "Background, design and evaluation of a conceptual framework for FLES curriculum." Pesola, C. (1995). (Doctoral Dissertation, University of Minnesota, 1995). *Dissertation Abstracts International, A 56* (12*)*, 4653, p. 88, (Reprinted with permission).

The curriculum of the ideal FLES model includes the use of technology. The term "technology" refers to a range of possibilities for the second language classroom. It includes,

> the low technology of the chalkboard and the old fashioned…bulletin board to the middle-range technology of overhead projectors, audio tapes, and videotapes to the high technology of Internet-based tasks, international e-mailing, "regular" computer-assisted instruction, and "intelligent" computer-assisted instruction (Oxford, 1998, p. 137).

Oxford also gave guiding principles for adopting a purposeful approach to the use of technology.

> Such instruction must have communicative competence as its cornerstone, provide appropriate language assistance tailored to the student, provide appropriate error correction suited to the student's changing needs over time, offer an abundance of authentic language input, provide interesting and relevant themes and meaningful language tasks, be designed for use by students with different learning styles, teach students to become better learners…use a variety of interaction types, and involve all language skills (p. 143).

Teachers in a FLES classroom may be overwhelmed by the thought of bringing technology into their teaching experiences, especially in classes with relatively short sessions. As we move more and more into a technology-based society, acceptance of the possibilities for classroom instruction will most likely grow.

Two FLES programs on Long Island, New York are incorporating technology components into the programs. In one program, limitations on time and conflicts with requirements for working with technology left FLES teachers with the option of entering into the computer labs with their students. The result was more positive than they originally expected. Another district sought a grant through the United States Department of Education's Foreign Language Assistance Program (FLAP). This funding is available for existing programs that seek to enhance the instructional experience. Funding is especially targeted for the use of technology. A three-year grant for three hundred thousand dollars was awarded to incorporate technology in the FLES program. Interdisciplinary activities using computers and the Internet are being developed and included in the FLES curriculum of this district. The department supervisor describes the program as follows:

> The East Islip Schools Elementary Foreign Language Improvement Program maximizes the benefits and capabilities offered through computer technology, the internet and e-mail, to assist students in building proficiency in Spanish and cultural comprehension while simultaneously achieving the New York State learning Standards in the other disciplines. Through collaboration with the New York Institute of Technology School of Education, East Islip teaching staff is becoming adept at integrating technology and language instruction in an interdisciplinary fashion. The program targeted all 4th graders in the first year, 5th graders this year and will target 6th graders next year. Students are carrying out math, science, language arts and technology projects in Spanish. The collaborative arrangement between NYIT and East Islip has resulted in unique curriculum and interdisciplinary program development that can be replicated in other schools around the nation (Hiller, E-mail correspondence, June 5, 2001).

In spite of the excitement generated by the potential for the application of high technology, there very little research available that specifically addresses the use of technology in a FLES classroom. One study of the use of computer assisted language learning in a FLES program in Iowa City Public Schools (Schrier & Fast, 1992) indicated that the dearth of useful software and lack of teacher training have limited the effectiveness of technology. At the same time, some educators are finding the nature of the connections made through the use of technology has given students an increased global awareness, allowing them to "reach around the world, learning first-hand about other cultures" (Peck & Dorricott, 1994, p. 13).

Joining the use of technology with the efforts to acquire another language may be helpful for the teacher in certain situations.

With the focus on language, communication, and culture in the national standards…foreign language teachers are continually searching for easier and better ways to access authentic materials and provide real-life experiences that will improve their students' language skills and increase their cultural knowledge. As the Internet transforms the way we communicate with the world, it is only natural that this technology should play a major role in the foreign language classroom (Leloup & Ponterio, 1998, p. 60).

Whether this tool is as easily applied in the FLES classroom still remains to be seen. Yet, it has great possibilities.

Oxford summarized a discussion of the usefulness of technology by stating the question is not, "Is the use of technology better than the non-use of technology for language learning? The question is more accurately stated as: Which forms of technological assistance enhance student learning with reference to particular learning goals?" (Owston, 1997; Oxford, 1998, p. 142).

The forms of technological assistance for teachers are quite extensive and should be part of a FLES program for the 21st century. This includes audiocassettes, videocassettes, satellite broadcasts, the Internet, (E-mail, listservs, websites), CD-ROMs, software, overhead projectors, etc. These formats may provide children with communicative opportunities that may not exist in their local communities. It is up to the teacher to make technology work for the FLES classroom.

- **Strong cultural component**

- **Instruction presented in the target language**

The concept of cultural knowledge has evolved for second language instruction. It is no longer a separate unit, with artifacts, dates, beliefs, and customs. The importance of developing cultural proficiency goes back to the discussion of attitude enhancement (see Section Three). A teacher who has a very strong background in the culture is a necessity for a strong and successful FLES program. "Because authentic communication relies on accurate cultural knowledge and understanding, cultural experiences in the elementary school must contribute to children's understanding of the people whose language they are studying" (Met & Rhodes, 1990).

The work of Seelye (1984) is often cited as a framework for developing a model for cultural proficiency. The goals include:

1. The sense or functionality of culturally conditioned behavior,

2. Interaction of language and social variables,

3. Conventional behavior in common situations,

4. Cultural connotations of words and phrases,

5. Evaluating statements about a society,

6. Researching another culture,

7. Attitudes towards other cultures (pp. 49-58).

If we hope to bring children to a higher level of understanding, appreciation, and acceptance of other cultures, they must be involved in more than songs or recipes.

Curtain & Pesola (1994) presented a discussion of the elementary foreign language classroom as a "favorable setting for introducing the child to the whole world of diversity" (p. 190). They mention the goals of multicultural education described by Gollnick (1980):

1. Promoting the strength and value of cultural diversity,

2. Promoting human rights and respect for those who are different from oneself,

3. Promoting alternative life choices for people,

4. Promoting social justice and equal opportunities for all people,

5. Promoting equity in the distribution of power among groups (pp. 1-17).

Curtain and Pesola (1994) explained that "language teachers...have a responsibility to plan lessons with sensitivity to the racial and ethnic diversity present in their classrooms and in the world in which their students live" (p. 192). Their work is remarkably comprehensive in scope and variety of activities for integrating content, culture, and language. Some of the activities mentioned are: inviting foreign visitors, learning and performing folk dances, celebrating holidays, field trips, inviting children to bring into class items from the target culture, skimming newspapers and magazines, literature from the target country, email connections, etc. (pp. 192-194).

Successfully developing cultural understanding is possible through careful hiring, program planning, curriculum development, staff development, and clearly outlined goals. The FLES teacher must seize the opportunity to engage students in positive experiences with the target culture. "The image of children as concrete learners who are motivated by imagination, feelings, experiences with concrete situations suggest culture instruction that focuses on experience rather than transmission of facts" (Pesola, 1995, p. 69). An administrator shared ideas on how to develop cultural understanding through FLES:

>-We are trying to develop cultural awareness by bringing native speakers into the program. We feel she brings the culture to the children through her life experiences, her knowledge, and her exciting and captivating manner.

While native speakers may have an advantage in cultural background, non-natives who have studied abroad and/or have maintained contact with people from the target culture (and acknowledge the importance of this concept) are able to engage students in concrete cultural learning experiences as well.

Whether a teacher is a native or non-native, the target language should be used almost exclusively during instruction. The previously held belief that elementary second language teachers do not need to use the language to a great degree is one of the reasons early second language programs failed in the 1960s (Curtain & Pesola, 1994). Presenting instruction in the target language as much as possible strengthens the language and cultural learning for the students. One FLES teacher explained,

>-At first I thought they would be lost, if I used only Spanish, but I find that they just expect it. I know I act things out a lot to help them understand, but I am always staying in the language, and it works.

- **Staff certified in FLES methodology**
- **Staff development and networking opportunities**

In order to teach in a FLES program in New York State, teachers must have 7-12 certification in the second language and an addendum for instruction of the second language at the elementary level. Elementary certified teachers with 7-12 certification in a second language may also teach in a FLES program with this addendum. There are some programs at universities or colleges in New York State where an elementary license may include foreign languages as one of the common branches.

FLES Certification is currently offered through several post secondary institutions nationwide. In New York State, the addendum on the 7-12 certification is obtained after completion of a 45-hour institute (see Dowling Certification Course, Appendix G). The certification courses focus on developing a knowledge base of instructional techniques that are appropriate for the elementary learner and are in alignment with theories on second language instruction. Without this course, secondary teachers may not be equipped to deal with the developmental issues for the elementary child. The elementary school teacher with certification in a second language also benefits from learning about current issues in second language instruction, specifically tailored for the young learner.

FLES teachers need to be aware of the professional organizations and support networks that serve them (see Appendix M). These professional organizations (CAL, NNELL, ACTFL, AATF, NYSAFLT, LILT) publish journals, hold conferences and special meetings, or provide data and networking opportunities for FLES teachers. Part of a budget for a FLES program should include monies for staff development as these opportunities should be provided on an on-going basis.

- **Language choice based on district's needs/interests**
- **Multiple entry points to study other languages (sixth grade, ninth grade)**

If the committee has representation from all areas of the instructional program, the language choice issue can be resolved through committee discussion. Foreign language teachers on the committee may share issues around articulation. Administrators may present ideas on staffing. Community members may represent interests of the community. The language choice should be based on the input of all key stakeholders to best serve the needs of the district. The best approach to language choice also includes options for entry into the study of other languages at other points in the program. This allows students to study additional languages, if their schedules allow, or they may decide to change from one language to another at these points (see also Section Eight, Choice of Language).

- **Plans for articulation with the middle school and high school**

    A FLES program cannot be sequential without a well-articulated continuation of study. The lessons from the FLES programs of the 1960s indicate how detrimental it is to a program to neglect this aspect. What does articulation mean? Articulation means the program has a seamless and carefully developed plan of connecting instruction both horizontally (within the elementary schools) and vertically (between the elementary, middle schools, and high schools). McClendon and Uchihara (1998) shared strategies for success in articulation of early second language programs.

    1. There must be collaborative curriculum and assessment development opportunities among teachers at different levels, along with opportunity for ongoing dialogue about program modifications for continual improvement in student achievement.

    2. All teachers in a K-12 foreign language program must understand the philosophy and goals at every level and must have opportunities to participate in in-service

activities which foster similar teaching strategies and approaches to instruction from level to level.

3. The National Standards will assist school systems in establishing a common ground for articulated program efforts. It is equally important that program objectives and goals, and the articulation plan developed to achieve them, be fully communicated to students, parents, and administrators (pp. 156-157).

These comprehensive plans will be difficult to sustain without starting them at the beginning. All committee members must have input into the articulation plan. What type of in-service will be offered? How often? When will teachers meet? Will they be given release time? The FLES team must address these, and many other issues.

Only one of the districts included in the interviews had developed a plan for articulation. Two of the districts mentioned ongoing meetings, and while they were not called "articulation" meetings, the content included some of these issues. In several of the districts the FLES teachers took it upon themselves to continue to meet to discuss the program and the progression of the students.

One of the problems that may arise by neglecting to address this issue is the repetition of the same material year after year. In one school district, a middle school teacher said,

>   -It was amazing to get the kids and have them speaking already. I know it was a good thing, but part of me felt sad that I didn't get to teach them the beginning anymore. I had to figure out where to start.

"Figuring out where to start," means the students must be on a continuum that registers the growth they experience. With some form of assessment or checklist of what the students are able to do, secondary teachers may adjust their teaching and curriculum. One leader in the field stated,

> -Nothing will turn a child off to the language more than having the whole year of instruction ignored, and starting all over again from scratch. How many times can you do that and not expect to lose the child?

- **Multiple assessment techniques (authentic assessment, report cards)**

The knowledge base of assessment in second language has grown along side of theory and practice across curriculum areas. Foreign language teachers are embracing the use of portfolios and performance-based assessment with their students. The National Standards for Foreign Language Learning stated,

> The development of standards has galvanized the field of foreign language education. The degree of involvement, and of consensus, among educators at all levels has been unprecedented…More than a decade of work on defining competency-based teaching and assessment focused language educators on preparing students who can use the language in meaningful ways, in real life situation" (1996, p.15).

While the National Standards for Foreign Languages represent the content or "what" of second language instruction, the ACTFL Performance Guidelines represent the "how well" (1999, p. 1). These guidelines are grouped into the following categories:

- comprehensibility

- comprehension

- language control

- vocabulary

- cultural awareness

- communication strategies

They establish a language for educators to use in the effort to assess, evaluate, and express where students are in the continuum of language learning.

Assessing the young language learner is not simply using shorter versions of what is used to assess students at later points in language learning. Developing purposeful assessments to demonstrate the proficiency achieved continues to be a challenge for early second language educators. Donato (1998) explained the complexities of developing sound assessment techniques for the young language learner. He presented a series of Socratic questions, intended to elicit reflection on the realities of creating valid and reliable measurements of second language ability. Some of his questions are:

-Do we have the knowledge to describe what novice, intermediate, and advanced child speakers can do, or are we committed to assessing children against adult performance by merely expanding descriptions of novice levels of foreign language proficiency?

-What assessment measures are best suited for young learners?

-How frequently should young learners be assessed…?

-Should formative alternative assessment that is linked to learning outcomes be our primary mode of assessment?

-Is there a role for formal summative assessment?

-How should assessments of the young language learner be used?

-For what other political, social, or ideological purposes could testing the early language learner and its results be used (Shohamy, 1997)?

Answers to some of these questions are presented in the on-going study of a Japanese FLES program (Donato, et al., 1996; 1994; Tucker, et al., 1995). The researchers focused much of their energy on the development of a meaningful assessment tool.

> We insisted upon assessment that allowed children to demonstrate what they knew rather than where they were deficient, and use a multiple assessment approach over time to describe a range of abilities…The picture to emerge was that assessing the young learner required multiple perspectives and that no single measure or test was capable of providing a profile of achievement and proficiency (p. 170).

While elementary teachers are accustomed to the use of portfolios and alternative assessment, FLES teachers are entering the field at a time when standardized testing and national standards beg the question, How are they doing, compared to others? At least one superintendent of a school district with a FLES program on Long Island expressed interest in some kind of standardized testing, some validation of what level of proficiency students were going to be able to attain. Currently, very few FLES programs are using any formal assessment; instead they are using informal assessment prepared by the teachers. A plan for multiple assessments, including authentic assessment and achievement tests where appropriate, should be developed to provide information on how students are progressing.

The FLES teachers interviewed also pointed to the use of the school report card as a validation of both the child's efforts and the effect of the program. Most of the districts with FLES programs include second language study as part of the students' report card.

The feedback is most often given in terms of a student's participation and effort (see Appendix J).

- **Program evaluation**

One of the reasons for the disappearance of FLES programs in the 1960s was the lack of program evaluation (Alkonis & Brophy, 1961; Curtain & Pesola, 1994). "Information from program evaluations is needed to determine the degree of success of early foreign language programs, as well as to identify factors contributing to or impeding that success" (Schinke-Llano, 1985, p. 47). Evaluation must attend to the model, goals, curriculum, staffing, and instructional approach of the program.

Program evaluations should be formative and summative, that is, there should be some type of evaluation of performance during the year and a summative evaluation administered at the end of the school year. The goal of developing communicative skills in the language can be assessed mid-year (formative). This would indicate the progress students have made towards that goal. Summative evaluations are assessments or surveys used at the end of an academic year (see sample summative evaluation in Section Fourteen). Information gathered from these instruments is used to make adjustments in instruction in the program for the following year (Schinke-Llano, 1985).

While assessment of students' abilities in the languages is important, an analysis of the program with a broader scope would allow for greater understanding of the successful aspects and the problematic areas. An instrument designed to gather data from all participants (students, classroom teachers, FLES teachers, administrators, and parents) would provide this type of analysis. "If evaluation takes place at all in a school district today, it tends to center on student and teacher performance" (Heining-Boynton, 1990, p. 432).

Heining-Boynton (1990) examined the issues around program evaluation in order to design a FLES Program Evaluation Instrument (FPEI). The instrument was piloted in Wake County Schools of North Carolina. Results from the pilot indicated strong support for the FLES program. Feedback from the survey also indicated the need for communication with and involvement of the classroom teacher for overall effectiveness of the program.

The FPEI has five sections, a survey for the FLES teachers, principals and administrators, classroom teachers, students and parents. The Likert scale format allows for easy tabulation and interpretation. It is easily adapted for use in any early second language program. "After administration and tabulation of the pilot test, the instrument was reexamined. As predicted, it took the respondents less than ten minutes to complete the forms" (p. 438). A copy of the FPEI is provided in Appendix K.

Since the cumulative effects of early foreign language instruction are usually not seen in a single academic year, program evaluation should continue for at least of three years (Schinke-Llano, 1985, p. 48). Schinke-Llano discussed other aspects of evaluation. Who will conduct the evaluation? Who will receive results of the evaluation? A teacher, chairperson, principal, or other administrators can administer the FPEI. Feedback from the evaluation could be shared with the board of education, PTA, teachers, administrators, and "when possible and appropriate, outcomes should be reported to state and national leaders and agencies" (Heining-Boynton, 1991, p. 197). A three-year program evaluation (using an instrument like the FPEI) combined with results from formative evaluation of student performance is necessary for the integrity of a strong FLES program.

- **Community support and public relations**

    In order to maintain support for an early foreign language program it is important to keep parents, teachers, administrators, and the original committee members informed about the progress and successes of the FLES program. While some districts do not establish a clear plan for publicity, many use newsletters to send updates to everyone involved, especially the parents (see Appendix L). Curtain and Pesola (1994, p. 275) provided a useful list of public relation activities,

    - Making use of the media to provide publicity

    - Taking field trips

    - Inviting parents and others to visit classes

    - Videotaping classes and specific class projects to share with parent groups and administrators

    - Reporting class activities to parents, to the principal, and to other teachers

    - Sending out a monthly newsletter

    - Taking part in school programs

    - Putting on a special program for parents and/or for the community

    - Sending second-language invitations and greeting cards as a class writing activity.

Lipton (1998, pp. 273-300) also shared a wealth of ideas for advocacy and public relations.

FLES teachers were asked if they did these types of activities. All of those

responding said they did several of the ones listed above. They did not consider it public

relations, but rather an extension of their teaching experience. Since this is not a typical

practice for second language teachers, follow-up questions were asked;

Why did you bother to do all this? Did it feel like extra work?

> -No, this is just part of this type of teaching. We automatically involve the kids in
>
> activities that bring us into their homes in one way or another.
>
> -The parents love it. They look forward to the play we do every year.
>
> -The newsletter helps me reinforce what I am doing with the kids at school. I
>
> send samples home through the newsletter and encourage the parents to practice
>
> with the kids. I think it is an extension of my teaching.

Section Seven

Effects of Implementing FLES Programs

This section of the document will present information on the additional benefits of FLES programs, based on research. The review of these studies is divided into five subsections: earlier studies of the effects of FLES programs on basic skills (1960-1977), more current studies of the effects on basic skills (1980-1997), studies of the effect of long term language study on SAT scores, studies of enhanced cognitive skills, and an effect size analysis of selected studies from this review.

Studies dating from the 1960s through the 1990s support the finding that FLES students outperform other students in assessments of basic skills such as reading, language arts, and math (Armstrong & Rogers, 1997; Campbell, 1963; District of Columbia Public Schools, 1971; Garfinkel & Tabor, 1991; Johnson et al., 1961, 1963; Lopato, 1963; Nespor, 1970; Offenberg, 1971; Rafferty, 1986; Sheridan, 1976). Other studies examined the effect of FLES programs on assessments of cognitive skills (Foster & Reeves, 1989; Landry, 1973,1974) and two studies examined the effect of long-term foreign language study on SAT results (Cooper, 1987; Eddy, 1981).

As state and national standards and assessments preoccupy the elementary school teacher, advocates for FLES programs must continue to analyze and document the effects of these programs on student achievement in areas other than foreign language. Teachers interviewed anecdotal evidence of the positive effects on the reading and language arts skills of the FLES students.

•Students are just more tuned into language in general.

•They seem to enjoy finding connections with other words.

•The phonetics of the language helps them to find patterns in English.

•All the practicing they do with listening is helping them with listening skills

in English, especially the fourth graders for the ELA exams.

Early Studies of Enhanced Basic Skills. One early study of a Long Island FLES program

(Campbell, 1962) supported the observations of the Long Island teachers interviewed.

The author found FLES students in grades one through three performed higher on tests of

reading, English language arts, math, and science than non-FLES students.

Another early study (Lopato, 1963) also examined a FLES program in a school

district of Long Island, New York. (This district has maintained a policy of FLES for

over 35 years.) In this study, two third-grade classes (the FLES group was the

experimental group and the non-FLES was the control group) were selected based on

geographic data to equate for socioeconomic background. Both classes took the Stanford

Achievement Test, Elementary Battery, Form J, at the beginning of the year and took

Form K at the end of the school year. The experimental group had significant gains in

math and spelling.

Johnson, Flores, & Ellison (1961) studied the effects of a FLES program on the

basic skills of third grade students in Illinois. The experimental group (FLES) had 23

students and the control group (non-FLES) had 17 students. The groups were equated for

IQ, age, and ability and no significant difference was found. The two groups were given

the Science Research Associates Achievement Series test to examine the effects of the

FLES program on basic skills. The results showed slight gains for the experimental

group in two of the seven areas assessed (computation and grammar). While these gains were not significant, the implication was that second language study did not have negative effects on basic skills.

Johnson et al. (1963) attempted to replicate their earlier study, this time with a larger sample size (47 experimental and 47 control). The IOWA test was used in this study and results showed insignificant gains again for the experimental group in vocabulary and reading. The authors concluded the program did not have a negative effect on performance of basic skills.

Several early studies of Latin FLES programs showed significant gains in tests of basic skills. Offenberg (1971) reported on a Latin FLES program in Philadelphia. The study examined the effects of the program on the vocabulary portion of the IOWA tests of Basic Skills. Thirty-four pairs of students from eight classes were included in the study. The authors stated the students were matched for SES by demographic data and for ability by the previous year's score on the IOWA test. The data was presented for the class as the unit of study. The class mean grade equivalent scores showed an increase of one year for the experimental group over the control group.

The District of Columbia Schools reported a study (1971) on the effects of a Latin, French, and Spanish FLES program. Scores on the Comprehensive Test of Basic Skills for 482 students were examined. Pretest and post-test scores were used for results after one year of second language study. Grade equivalent scores were presented to express the mean scores. In all three areas examined (vocabulary, comprehension, and reading) the Latin, French, and the Spanish FLES groups had significant gains over the non-FLES group.

Sheridan (1976) studied the effects of a Latin FLES program on scores on the Metropolitan Achievement Test. The MAT test was used as a pretest and post-test to examine differences after each year of study. Data from test results were presented for two years. The sample included 432 students (339 FLES in the experimental group, 93 non-FLES in the control group) for the second year. The sample for the third year was 359 students (248 experimental, 111 control).

Results from the second year of the program showed significant gains for the FLES students in word knowledge, math, science, math concepts, spelling, and math computation. The results from the third year showed gains in all areas for the experimental groups. Overall, the results seem to indicate an advantage for FLES student over non-FLES students on most areas of the MAT.

More Recent Studies of Enhanced Basic Skills. The most current studies of the effect of FLES programs on basic skills (such as reading, math, and language arts) claim the following: (1) FLES students (of average ability) score higher on achievement tests in reading than non-FLES students (Garfinkel & Tabor, 1991), and (2) FLES students score higher on achievement tests in English language arts, reading and math than non-FLES students (Armstrong & Rogers, 1997; Rafferty, 1986).

The purpose of Garfinkel & Tabor's study (1991) was to compare English reading scores of third and fourth-grade FLEX students studying Spanish with FLES students who extended the study of Spanish into grades five and six (p. 375). The setting of this study was a school district in Michigan. In this district, the third and fourth-grade students receive twenty minutes of instruction in Spanish twice a week for nine weeks. In grades five and six, students were able to extend their study of Spanish to one or two full years (twice a week for twenty-five minutes in fifth grade and three times a week for sixth grade).

The four-year study included 513 students. No significant difference was found between groups. The role of intelligence was tested by dividing the students into three groups, students of average intelligence (102 and below on the SAI), above average (103-114), and high level intelligence (115 and above on the SAI). The "mid-range scores were eliminated from the analysis...to make the contrast of intelligence scores more clearly visible" (p. 378). In addition, special education children were not included in the study. The results indicated that the students from the average ability group who continued with a second year of FLES had positive gains on the SAT reading test.

The implication of this finding was "foreign language study gives students of average intelligence a kind of enrichment they may not be getting from other studies or experiences" (p. 379). The discussion also focused on the quality of the model provided as impacting on the results. The model employed in this district focuses on language mastery, the use of authentic materials, meaningful and contextualized topics, whole brain-oriented procedures, and TPR (total physical response) techniques.

Armstrong & Rogers' study (1997) also highlighted the importance of the instructional model on the effects of the program.

Although the relationship of foreign language instruction to basic skills acquisition has been investigated regularly during the last 40 years, most published studies have attempted to quantify the effects...without addressing in any depth the nature of the instruction of the target language (p. 20).

The model for their study was a Spanish FLES program, meeting three times a week for 30 minutes. The focus of the instruction was meaningful communication, using TPR, and content from the five subject areas of the elementary curriculum.

Their study of 90 students in two elementary schools in Kansas had a control group (non-FLES students) and an experimental group (FLES students). The students were given the Metropolitan Readiness Test (MAT 7) as a pretest and post-test. The test gave scores for reading comprehension, math, and language and the posttest scores were used as dependent variables. In analyzing the effect of the independent variables (control or experiment group), the pretest scores, gender, and IQ were used compared to see if they were different groups. The analysis showed no difference for gender or IQ.

Further analysis showed there were significant differences between groups on the language and math areas of the tests. The reading comprehension scores did not show a significant difference. The authors concluded the results support the findings of other studies which claim early second language study facilitates the learning of language arts (Rafferty, 1986).

Rafferty (1986) conducted a statewide study of 13,200 Louisiana students in third, fourth, and fifth grade (scores on the Louisiana Basic Skills test in math and language arts). The analyses showed that regardless of race, sex, or grade level, FLES students outperformed the non-FLES students in the language arts tests.

> Foreign language study appears to increase the scores of boys as much as girls, and blacks as much as other races. This finding supports the notion that, beginning as early as the third grade, second language study facilitates the acquisition of minimum skills in the native tongue (p .11).

The findings also indicated an advantage for the fifth grade that more than doubled the FLES students. The fifth grade FLES students also outperformed the non-FLES students in math skills.

These three studies are cited often in the literature on FLES. They support the theory that second language study has a positive effect on learning in other subject areas. The Armstrong & Rogers study (1997) gave the most details regarding the features of the FLES model. This information is important since certain aspects of the models of instruction may affect the outcomes.

Effect of Long term Second Language Study on SAT Scores. Eddy (1981) examined the foreign language-SAT relationship of students from three high schools in Maryland. One of the research questions, "Do students who have studied a foreign language for a lengthy period score better on the SAT-Verbal than students who have studied foreign language for a shorter period?" (p. 56) is pertinent to the present discussion.

The findings indicated a positive relationship between the between the length of study of a foreign language and the verbal scores on the SAT. Other findings were: studying two foreign languages had no significant effect on SAT scores, the language chosen had no effect on SAT scores, and higher grades on report cards for the foreign language class increased the effect on the SAT score. The implication from this study is allowing for a longer period of second language study (i.e. beginning foreign languages at the elementary school level) may have the best result on later performance on high stakes testing.

Cooper (1987) replicated the Eddy study, examining the foreign language-SAT relationship in a random sample of 1,778 students from a large metropolitan area in the

Southeast. The student sample was drawn from ten high schools with a majority of white students and eight high schools with a majority of black students. Overall SAT performance in the district was in the above average range. All students in the study had taken the SAT and the CAT tests.

Cooper found foreign language students scored significantly higher on the SAT than non-foreign language students, and SAT verbal scores increased with each half year of foreign language study. The implications of this study are that the skills developed in foreign language study enhance performance on tests of ability, like the SAT tests and the greater the length of study, the greater the effect on scores.

The College Board (1992) also showed a correlation of length of study of a foreign language with higher scores. The mean verbal and math scores for all students were 423 and 476, respectively. The mean verbal and math scores for students who had studied a foreign language were 471 and 523, respectively (ERIC Review, 1998, p. 5).

Since standardized test scores receive a great deal of attention in our society, the findings of these studies are meaningful. Their findings imply that the greater the number of years of study of a foreign language, the greater the achievement may be on SAT tests. Starting second language study in the elementary grades may have the added benefit of increased scores on standardized tests.

Studies of Enhanced Cognitive Skills. The cognitive benefits of bilingualism have been well-documented in the research on language minority students (Bamford & Mizokawa, 1991; Bruck, et al., 1974; Cummins, 1976, 1981; Hakuta, 1986; Weatherford, 1986). A definition of cognitive ability is "the thinking process engaged in the act of acquiring knowledge" (Webster's Dictionary, 1989, p. 287). Several studies of FLES programs show cognitive gains for students on tests of cognitive skills such as evaluation, error detection, and creative thinking (Foster & Reeves, 1989; Landry, 1974).

The goal of many educational programs is to provide students with the opportunity to enhance their thinking skills. Landry's studies (1973, 1974) are often cited as support for the theory that early second language provides this opportunity. Landry's conceptual framework reflects Vygotsky's theory of language learning. He stated, "Second language learning appears…not only to provide children with the ability to depart from the traditional approaches to a problem but also to supply them with possible rich resources for new and different ideas" (1973, p. 111).

The first of his two studies (1973) examined the effect of a FLES program on two components of creative thinking (figural fluency and figural flexibility). The 48 students (from grades four through six) in the study were equated for IQ and age. No significant differences between the groups were found. The scores for students in the FLES program were compared with students not in the program. The results on the Torrance Test of Creative Thinking showed a significant difference for the FLES students over the non-FLES students. In examining each dependent variable separately, the analysis showed significant increases in figural fluency and figural fluency.

The purpose of Landry's study (1974) was to compare the development of creative or divergent thinking for FLES and non-FLES students. The sample included 224 students, selected randomly from six schools in New Hampshire. The students were from first grade (64), fourth grade (80), and sixth grade (80). The same test of creative thinking (Torrance Test of Creative Thinking) was administered to the students at each grade level. After five years of language study, significant differences between the FLES and non-FLES groups were found for the sixth graders.

Foster & Reeves (1989) using other tests of cognitive processing also measured enhanced cognitive skills. The Ross test of Higher Cognitive Processes measures the ability to analyze, synthesize, and evaluate data. The Butterflies and Moths Error Detection Table measures the metacognitive skill of comprehension monitoring. In this study, four groups were formed of 67 sixth grade students in a school in Louisiana. One group was the control group (non-FLES) and the others were the experimental groups (FLES). The students received 30 minutes of French daily. The teachers used the communicative approach to instruction, focusing on meaningful, contextualized language.

The study found that FLES groups scored significantly higher that the non-FLES students in three areas:

(1) evaluation skills, (2) total score of all cognitive functions on the Ross test, and (3) the comprehension monitoring skill. A linear trend analysis indicated a relationship of performance with increased number of months of study.

This study supports the findings of the Landry studies of the cognitive benefits of early and long-term second language study. All three studies indicate FLES programs offer the added benefit of enhancing the cognitive development of young children.

Summary

The research reviewed in this section seems to indicate there are benefits to beginning second language study early, in addition to the attitudinal and language proficiency benefits cited in Section Four of this document. These academic and cognitive benefits present powerful rationales for including FLES in an already crowded elementary curriculum. Many opponents of FLES argue for the urgency to complete existing curriculum requirements and meet standards for success on state assessments. However, since FLES programs aid in developing the reading and language arts skill of students, the policy of early second language study is viable and important. The Russian psychologist Vygotsky explained,

> Goethe clearly saw it when he wrote that he who knows no foreign language does not truly know his own. One may say that the knowledge of the foreign language stands to that of the native one in the same way as knowledge of algebra stands to knowledge of arithmetic, enhancing it and turning it into a concrete application of algebraic laws. The child's approach to language becomes more abstract and generalized…the acquisition of foreign language…liberates him [sic] from the dependence on concrete linguistic forms and expressions (Vygotsky, 1986, p. 160).

Section Eight

Obstacles and Challenges to Implementing a FLES Program

Some of the difficulties or obstacles encountered while implementing a FLES

policy are outlined in this section. The areas discussed are: negative effects on other

subject areas, finding time in the school day, staffing, scheduling, choice of model

(FLEX, FLES, or immersion), choice of language(s), deciding at which grade level to

start, and the costs of the program.

Negative Effects. As FLES programs grew rapidly throughout the 1960s, critiques and

resistance stemmed from the concern that students would be missing out on precious

instructional time for the core curricula areas. (This concern continues to be voiced

today.) Researchers tested the reality of this fear by examining performance in regular

subject areas of students in FLES programs against non-FLES students.

Several studies indicate there are no negative effects of a FLES program (Leino &

Haak, 1963; McCaig, 1988; Potts, 1967). These studies were conducted to assess

whether time taken away from the elementary curriculum resulted in lower performance

for the FLES students in other subject areas. Leino & Haak (1963) examined the effect

of grade level on achievement in Spanish (were the children in sixth grade able to learn

more Spanish than the children in fourth grade), the effect of IQ on foreign language

learning, and the effect of deletion of time from subject areas to learn Spanish. Classes

from twelve schools were involved in a three-year study of the effect of a Spanish FLES

program on achievement in other subject areas.

The program designers created the tests used (to assess the learning of Spanish).

The IOWA Basic Skills Test was used to test vocabulary, reading, language, work-study skills, and arithmetic. The Stanford Social Studies Test was used to assess learning in history, geography, and civics. Researchers used the Otis Beta Intelligence test as a measure of IQ. Students in the control group were exposed to 75 minutes of instruction per week in Spanish for three years.

The study seems to suggest that for all subject areas, for all grades, in each year, there was no negative effect on performance in other subjects due to the deletion of time for second language study. In fact, FLES students had an advantage in language arts.

Potts (1967) built on the Leino & Haak study, by focusing on the possible negative effects of a FLES program on reading skills. Forty-three first graders and 37 second graders from a school district in upstate New York were selected at random to form an experimental group (FLES) and control group (non-FLES). The California Test of Mental Maturity was administered as a measure of mental age (both language and non-language mental age). The California Achievement Test and The California Reading Test were used to assess students at the end of the year.

The experimental group received 15 minutes of instruction in French daily, using the audio-lingual method (a method of choice during the 1960s). This approach focuses on repetition of dialogue and pronunciation through cassettes and teacher initiation. The control group received an equal amount of instruction in dance.

The results indicate no significant difference due to the FLES instruction. However, the study also shows that the FLES program had no negative effect on the reading ability of the children. One important note is the quality of the FLES program. It is possible that if the program were of a different nature, more communicative, or using content from the elementary curriculum (content-based instruction), the author may have seen different results, possibly an advantage for the FLES students.

The most recent study of the effects of a FLES program with similar findings is the McCaig study (1988). The purpose of the study was to examine the effects of a FLES program on language arts skills and attitudes. This four-year study involved third and fourth graders from seven different schools in Michigan. Four of the schools had FLES programs. Three of the schools did not. Students were matched for IQ using the Test of Cognitive Skills. District tests were used to analyze performance in the language arts. Comparisons were made for students grouped into high ability (IQ above 110), average ability (IQ 90-109), and low ability (IQ below 90).

Statistical analysis indicated there was no significant difference for children from all abilities from the experimental or control groups. The findings indicated there was neither a benefit nor detrimental effect of the FLES program. The study also included a survey of student interest in continuing with the study of a foreign language. The results indicate FLES students were more likely to continue with the study of the language in tenth grade than students who started studying the language at the junior high school level.

These studies support the theory that second language study does not interfere with learning in other subjects. Some of the results indicated a slight advantage for the FLES students.

Finding time in the school day. The issue of not having enough time in the school day is often noted as one of the major objections to a policy of FLES (Baranick & Markham, 1986). Some people express concerns about taking time from other subject areas in order to allow for the foreign language class. However, reviews of research on FLES refute concerns about low academic performance due to lost academic learning time (Donoghue, 1965, 1969, 1981; Eddy, 1978; Masciantonio, 1977; Mavrogenes, 1970).

Questions about the "main obstacles to implementing early second language study" were asked of personnel from school districts with FLES programs, as well as those without FLES programs. The most common response was the difficulty in finding time in the elementary school day. Table 8 summarizes how the districts with FLES programs overcame this obstacle.

Table 8

Time Found in School Day for FLES Programs

Time was taken from regular class session	5
Time was added to school day	4
Time was taken from another program	2
Time was considered review of content area from curriculum (content-related instruction)	2

Several districts took advantage of the opportunity to extend the school day in order to introduce a FLES program. For example, some of these districts began school at 9:00 am. The community sought an earlier start, or the district was considering lengthening the day for increased instructional time. This discussion coincided with the interest in starting a FLES program. It made the implementation of the program easier for these districts by moving the starting time to 8:30 am (or adding 15 minutes to the end of the day).

In two of the districts, time was specifically reduced in the language arts segment of the day (as there was time for extended reading). The belief that foreign language study reinforced language skills provided a rationale for reducing time in this area. Most of the districts expected classroom time to be "adjusted" without specification of exactly how, or from what subject area. Teachers interviewed claimed the classroom teachers "clipped" minutes from various segments of their day to allow for the visiting FLES teacher.

Two districts "added" to academic instruction time by implementing a content-related instruction FLES program. Through this approach, the elementary curriculum is reinforced thematically by the FLES teacher. For example, if the classroom is presenting a lesson on butterflies to her second grade class, the FLES teacher would present a lesson in the target language, also based on the butterfly. This method provides a new rationale for the FLES policy, one that resembles immersion, which is an opportunity for the students to relearn or to experience the same concepts in a different modality.

The classroom teachers were most vocal in the school districts included in this policy analysis regarding their diminished instructional time before the programs were initiated. A majority of the FLES teachers interviewed (90%) said the partner classroom teachers became advocates of the program within one year. The FLES teachers stated the reasons for the new-found support of the classroom teachers were: the enthusiasm of the students, how rapidly they seem to learn, and the positive effects on learning in other areas. In one school district, the classroom teachers became so motivated by the FLES

class that they sought staff development on learning the language themselves.

While finding time in the school day was mentioned as the most challenging

obstacle, all of the administrators interviewed felt it was best resolved by including

classroom teachers in the discussions, or by employing a content-related approach. Table

9 provides a sample schedule for a third grade class. This class is involved in a FLES

program that meets three times a week for forty minutes.

Table 9

Sample Elementary Schedule with FLES

Monday	Tuesday	Wednesday	Thursday	Friday
	9:15 Computers			
		10:15 Library	9:45	9:55 FLES
10:30 Art	10:40 FLES		10:35 Computers	10:30 Remedial Reading
11:30 Remedial Reading	11:30 Remedial Reading			
12:00 L	U	N	C	H
	1:15 Gym		1:15 Gym	1:15 Music
		1:40 FLES		
2:30 ESL	2:30 ESL		2:30 ESL	

Staffing. How can school districts staff a FLES program if most districts do not currently

have sufficient numbers of teachers to fulfill additional requirements in foreign language

(Comments of the New York State Commissioner of Education on the Report of the Foreign Language Implementation Committee, 1998)? In nine of the thirteen school districts with early elementary, sequential FLES programs on Long Island, the teachers were found from within the district.

Secondary teachers of the target language were asked to teach the FLES classes, or they initiated the program themselves. Two of the districts that hired new staff found teachers from out-of-state. Several of the teachers were elementary school teachers who also had certification in the second language. Most of these teachers (from within and without of the district) did not hold a special certification for elementary foreign language instruction prior to teaching in the program.   One option for hiring teachers for a FLES program might be to share staff across districts. Neighboring districts might more easily hire staff to teach FLES in their programs if they can share part time positions with other districts.

In order to teach foreign languages at the elementary school level in New York State, the following requirements must be met: (1) the teacher must hold 7-12 certification in the second language, and (2) the teacher must obtain an extension for this certification through a state approved, 45-hour FLES methodology course. Elementary school teachers who also have certification in the second language and or a certification in Bilingual Education may also teach in a FLES program.

Scheduling. Several questions arose in discussions with educators regarding scheduling for FLES. How much time is necessary? Is it better to meet more often for fewer minutes each session or for fewer days for more time?

The scheduling of elementary school foreign language programs will depend to a large extent on the program model selected and the goals established for it…No type of quality product can be expected from an investment in instruction of less than thirty minutes daily (Armstrong, 1998, p. 229).

The time allotted for instruction in FLES programs analyzed for this document ranges from 30 to 120 minutes per week. Some of these programs are evolving, with plans for more time or more days. All of the teachers interviewed felt it was better to meet with students more frequently for less time than for fewer days for longer periods of time, but that the total number of minutes should not be less than 60 minutes per week.

Leaders in the field have recommended a guideline for scheduling an effective FLES program as meeting at least every other day for a minimum of seventy-five minutes per week (Curtain & Pesola, 1994; Rosenbusch, 1992). The Performance Guidelines for K-12 Learners (1999), prepared by the American Council on the Teaching of Foreign Languages states, "Considering the content and intended K-12 sequence set forth in the Standards for Foreign Language Learning… accomplishment of such content standards required students to be enrolled in elementary programs that meet from 3-5 days per week for no less than 30-40 minutes per class (p. 6)." Based on this framework, this organization has established a visual representation of "Anticipated Performance Outcomes" (see Appendix F). This chart depicts the variation in achievement expected with a longer sequence of second language study.

In an effort to connect scheduling with the issue of where to find the time in the school day, foreign language educators were asked to share sample schedules for 90 and 120 minute FLES programs models. Table 10 shows a schedule for one of the FLES teachers. This teacher employs content-related instruction to assist the classroom teacher

in delivering and supporting the elementary curriculum. In one of the programs, the

school district integrates art and computer with the FLES program to maintain the time

commitment established for each area.

Table 10

Sample Schedule for FLES Teacher   (FLES= three times a week)

Monday	Tuesday	Wednesday	Thursday	Friday
9:15 4th (A)	9:15 4th (A)	Prep		9:15 3rd (A)
	10:00 3rd (A)	10:15 5th (A)	9:45 5th (B)	9:55 3rd (B)
10:30 4th (B)	10:40 3rd (B)	11:00 5th (B)	10:35 5th (A)	10:30 4th (A)
11:10 Special Ed. Class				
12:00 L	U	N	C	H
1:15 5th (A)	Prep	1:05 3rd (A)		Prep
2:00 5th (B)	2:00 4th (B)	1:40 3rd (B)		Prep
		2:15 4th (B)		

3(A), 3(B)= 2 third grade classes; 4(A), 4(B)= 2 fourth grade classes; 5(A), 5(B)= 2 fifth

Choice of Model (FLEX, FLES, Immersion). The focal model of this document has been

the Sequential FLES model. As mentioned above, FLES models may vary in the amount

of time allowed for instruction. Leaders in the field of FLES have established a

minimum of 75 minutes per week as a guideline (Rosenbusch, 1992). It is common sense

to deduce that "the level of language fluency a student will gain in an elementary school

foreign language class is directly related to the amount of time students spend learning

the language, and on the intensity of that language experience" (Curtain & Pesola, 1994,

p. 256). Table 11 highlights a comparison of early language programs.

Table 11

Comparison of Early Language Program Models

FLEX	(Sequential) FLES	Immersion
Goals include cultural awareness and limited language proficiency	Goals include a degree of language and cultural proficiency and may include reinforcing elementary curriculum	Goals include a substantial degree of proficiency in the target language and culture and to master content taught in target language
Study of one or more languages	Study of one language with multiple entry into other languages offered	Study of one language for a long sequence
1 - 2 times a week, for 15-30 minutes	3-5 times a week for 20 - 30 minutes	50 % - 100 % of the school day is offered in target language
Usually a push-in program, sometimes done through videos or classroom teacher	Usually a push-in program with FLES teachers as the "specialists"	Teachers use target language in regular classroom instruction

Some comments about choosing the FLES model from the interviews are:

Superintendent:

-I believe the best model is immersion, but we would never get the staff needed,

and it would be such an extensive change, I doubt we would get the support of all

95

parties. I believe the best way to go about this, and to offer a rigorous FLES program, if not immersion, is to hire bilingual elementary teachers.

Foreign Language Chairperson:

-The model we went with (FLES) is working well and it is the most practical for us. We already had the teacher on staff, they just had to find the time in the elementary school day, and they did.

Teacher:

-We went with what the research said. It made sense to us. Of course, I would like to see the kids get more language, but honestly, I don't think they are ready to hire another teacher, and I couldn't handle anymore classes.

Teacher:

-We first visited other districts, to see what their model was like. The FLES model was the most popular and it was easy to apply to our school.

Rhodes (1989) discussed the implications of program choice among FLES, FLEX and immersion;

> Knowing what we know about proficiency levels attainable by immersion students and FLES students, a fundamental question arises concerning the general issue of what kind of programs to recommend to schools across the country. If we are striving to attain language competence for all Americans, is it better to offer limited exposure to many children (FLES) or intensive exposure to fewer children (immersion)? The question can first be addressed by investigating state and national foreign language initiatives and priorities to find out exactly what the overall language goals are for K-12 students. Then, the goals and limitations of

both types of programs should be evaluated so recommendations can be made to school districts as to how best to optimally design language programs at the elementary school level (p. 55-56).

The proficiency guidelines for the instruction of foreign languages throughout the nation (prepared by the American Council of Teachers of Foreign Languages) assume that school districts will provide regular FLES or immersion programs with instruction at the middle school level and the equivalent of four units of credit at the high school level (ACTFL, Proficiency Guidelines, Draft, 1998). If we examine the mandates recommended by the Commissioner's Foreign Language Implementation Committee for New York State Schools (1998), we can see that the goal of all students meeting Checkpoint B proficiency (i.e. passing the Second Language Regents Examination) at the high school level will be more easily met by the implementation of Sequential or intensive FLES programs in our schools.

In choosing a program model (FLES, FLEX, or immersion), school districts must consider the purpose for implementing such a program. The distinction set among these types of programs is that immersion allows for at least 50% of the core curriculum to be taught in the foreign language. In FLES programs, a maximum of 5-20% of the day is devoted to foreign language study with the focus on studying the language itself. The goal of FLEX programs is usually to develop an appreciation of other cultures, and instruction may be offered as little as a few weeks out of the school year.

If the attainment of a substantial degree of proficiency in the language is the goal, it is logical that the more exposure afforded by the program, the greater the benefits. This reasoning would be the basis for selecting immersion as the program model since it would allow for the greatest exposure to the language. Yet, program choice is more complex than the intended purpose alone. Decisions regarding program choice involve many issues, such as: funding, teacher availability, articulation issues, community needs and preferences, space, materials, student population, etc. (Orringer, 1998).

The findings of the studies on the comparison of the three types of early language programs are: (1) immersion is the most effective program for the development of skills in the second language (Campbell et al., 1985; Rhodes et al., 1989; Riddick, 1991), (2) (Sequential) FLES programs do provide students with the opportunity to develop measured success in second language skills (Campbell et al., 1985, Rhodes et al., 1989; Riddick, 1991), (3) intensive FLES programs (30 minutes, 5 times a week) are more effective than less rigorous models of FLES in developing skills in the second language (Rhodes et al., 1989), and, (4) most of the successful early second language programs in New York State are FLES models (Zlokower, 1991).

While the research clearly shows support for immersion models in terms of linguistic gains, there are drawbacks to this model. An immersion program, while offering the highest level of proficiency, would require all elementary school teachers (including art, music, and physical education) to have near-native ability in the language taught. This would also necessitate the purchasing of materials across the curriculum in the target language (Tucker et al., 1995). The intense commitment of time and resources for immersion programs may not be possible for most school districts.

A FLEX program is the least costly since it can be implemented for a very short time period and with little interruption to the daily schedule. This type of program requires the hiring of very few language specialists. In some districts videos are used or the classroom teacher provides the instruction using a limited knowledge of the target language and culture. The main disadvantages to this model are that it does not allow for the development of language skills and it is not part of an articulated sequence (Hoch, 1998).

The available research on FLES models shows that it can allow for substantial development of language skills and cultural awareness. It is easier and less expensive to start up than an immersion program. Materials used in a FLES program are often teacher-prepared so cost in this area is relatively low. Intensive FLES programs (language taught 5 days a week for 30 minutes) provide students with the opportunity to develop greater linguistic achievement than less rigorous FLES models or a FLEX program (Heining-Boynton, 1998; Rhodes, 1989). A strong argument for choosing FLES as the model relies on the premise that most school districts would be able to implement a Sequential FLES program with reasonable cost and planning. (A cost analysis is presented later in this Section.)

One of the first studies to deal with the effect of one program model over another was done by Gray et al. (1984). The Campbell et al. study (1985) was a revised version of the same study. In this study, the researchers were interested in discovering how participation in immersion, partial immersion or FLES would affect student performance on a language achievement instrument. The sample included 382 elementary students from fifteen schools across the nation involved in immersion, partial immersion or FLES programs. The methods involved administration of a language assessment instrument (the MLA test) to measure achievement in French or Spanish. The results showed greatest achievement for the immersion students, followed by the partial immersion students and then FLES students.

The test had four subsections (listening, speaking, reading and writing) and mean percentile scores were compared for the three groups in all sections of the test. The mean percentile scores for these four sections for the French FLES students were 14, 43, 22 and 9, respectively. The French immersion students had mean percentiles of 80, 99, 77 and 40. The mean scores for the Spanish FLES students were 22, 65, 14, and 16. The Spanish immersion students outperformed the FLES students in this language as well with mean percentile scores of 88, 99, 75, and 69. (The partial immersion scores fell between the FLES and the immersion scores.)

While, at face value, this study appears to support an argument in favor of immersion programs, the important inference is that, with a clearly stated goal, FLES students can achieve some degree of language proficiency desired by the school district. "It should not be overlooked that the students in the French FLES programs do benefit from the study of a second language. [The FLES students] did perform at the 45th percentile for speaking" (Gray et al., p. 27). The mean speaking score for Spanish FLES had a percentile of 65, indicating that these students performed as well or better than 65 percent of students with no FLES experience. "Students in the FLES programs …performed relatively well on oral proficiency. It is not surprising that they were unable to perform well on the reading and writing subtests given their limited exposure to these skills" (p. 56).

In a similar study, Rhodes et al. (1989) examined proficiency levels of students involved in immersion vs. FLES programs. (FLEX models were excluded because of the lack of attention to linguistic development in these models.) They also collected (qualitative) data to explain the variation in similar types of programs. The results indicate immersion is the strongest model for developing linguistic proficiencies in the second language. They also show intensive FLES (5 times a week for 30 minutes) is more effective than regular FLES (2-5 times a week for 15-30 minutes).

The sample included fifth and sixth graders from nine elementary school language programs. There were 85 immersion students, 75 FLES students and 265 FLEX students. The FLEX students were included only in the results of an attitude questionnaire as their language proficiency was not developed enough to assess them on language achievement tests.

The three instruments used were the CLEAR Oral Proficiency Exam (COPE), which focuses on communicative competency, an attitudinal questionnaire "What do YOU think?" (Gardner & Smythe, 1974; Snow, 1985), and a test for FLES students, the FLES Test-Spanish (Thompson, et al., 1988). (The FLES test evaluates listening and reading comprehension skills.) The mean raw scores on the COPE test reveal that the immersion students outperformed the FLES students by more than four to one. The immersion total raw scores (out of 36) ranged from 21.42 to 27.11. In contrast, the FLES scores ranged from 2.88 to 4.58.

The results revealed that the type of program proved to be a significant source of variation. The immersion students outperformed the FLES students in all four sub-skills assessed by the COPE (comprehension, fluency, vocabulary and grammar). Performance for all groups, including FLES and immersion students, was strongest in comprehension, and then decreased in strength so that grammar was the weakest skill.

The analysis showed that immersion programs had greater variation than FLES programs. The differences in similar program types were attributed to specific design features, little turnover in administration, longevity of the program, parental support, articulation efforts and the number of hours of instruction. These data were collected through interviews, visitations, observations and documentation.

Scores for the FLES Test also favored the immersion students, with the type of program as a significant source of variation. Scores for the immersion schools ranged from 67.65 to 68.92. FLES scores ranged from 56.25 to 59.42. There was no significant difference for immersion schools, as would be expected, because the FLES test could not discriminate for performance at the high end. A significant level of difference was found in program variation for the FLES models when they were subdivided into intensive FLES programs and regular FLES programs, with intensive FLES students achieving higher scores. The intensive FLES met five days a week for 30 minutes a day. The regular FLES met either a half-hour or one hour a day, two days a week or 22 minutes a day for five days a week.

Rhodes concluded that the amount and intensity of instruction, along with other factors particular to the school district (such as staff, parental encouragement, content-based instruction, etc.) strongly influence the outcomes for proficiency in the second language.

Riddick (1991) did another comparison of student performance in partial immersion and FLES programs. Riddick's research questions were:

Are students who study math, science, and social studies through a second language hampered when compared with their non-immersion peers? Does intensive study of a second language interfere with native language usage? Is

partial immersion more effective than FLES in producing fluency in the second

language? (p. 14).

She examined student performance on California Achievement Tests (CAT), the North

Carolina third grade tests for science and social studies and the FLES Test-French. The

CTB-McGraw Hill Test of Cognitive Skills was used for IQ comparisons.

The population of the study was the third grade class of 1989-1990 at an

elementary school in Gates County, North Carolina. These 57 students were involved in

either an intensive FLES program or a partial immersion program. The racial

composition of the groups in the partial immersion program was 40% African American

and 60% white. In the FLES program the population was 60% African American and

40% white. The school district is described as a small, rural system with few or limited

resources and a relatively low SES (50% of the students receive free or reduced breakfast

and lunch).

The socioeconomic feature of the school district distinguishes this study from

other studies of FLES programs where the children are from middle to upper class

families. Performance on standardized tests for children in a special program may be

expected to be higher than those outside of the program. Many documented FLES

programs are found in areas with many resources, in magnet schools or areas where there

was some exposure to a second language in the subculture of the community (Riddick,

1991, p. 16).

The results show that there was no difference in academic achievement that

correlates to either program. The immersion group scored significantly higher than the

FLES group in French listening skills after adjusting for SES and IQ. The FLES group

scored significantly higher that the immersion group in social studies. The results show

that the FLES or the partial immersion programs did not affect achievement in the

elementary curricula areas (science, math, and reading). This would support the

argument that intensive FLES programs can be as effective as partial immersion

programs since the achievement scores for students from both groups are comparable.

The only area of difference was the higher performance in listening skills for the

immersion students.

In a qualitative study of FLEX, FLES and immersion programs, Zlokower (1991),

examined trends and issues in program implementation in thirteen school districts in New

York State. The study involved interviews, visitations and documentation of data on the

programs. She stated,

> According to all relevant information on this issue of elementary language
>
> implementation, the most limited cautious approach, early on allows for steady
>
> expansion in incremental stages. Those programs (FLES) that have lasted for
>
> decades mainly offer frequent lessons of minimal duration, and often in only one
>
> language, or at upper elementary grade levels (p. 211).

In a discussion of expansion predictions Zlokower states, "the FLES model... will be the

mode of the immediate future. These models provide opportunities for limited

implementation, in grade level, lesson time, and frequency of instruction. They also

offer the option of a limited initial staff" (p. 224-225).

In summarizing these findings, it appears, from the results of the studies presented

that "more is better" as far as language proficiency is concerned. The ideal program for foreign language instruction at the elementary school level would be one that allows for maximum exposure and instruction in the content areas. School districts that have implemented second language programs at the elementary level have decided the regular (or intensive) FLES model is the most effective and realistic model. It provides enough of an opportunity for language development and a reasonable implementation plan.

Choice of Language(s). Once a committee is established, research is underway, and the committee members are meeting regularly to analyze the issues, the choice of language must be addressed. Educators from school districts with (or planning to implement) FLES programs were asked, "How did you choose the language(s) to offer?" Some of their responses are listed below:

-We surveyed the parents, and they said they wanted Spanish.

-We went with Mandarin Chinese because of the teachers that were available and the desire to be boldly different.

-Spanish is the second most spoken language in our community.

-It was a "top-down" decision.

-We went with the teacher who was available.

-The community and the committee felt Spanish was the most useful language.

-We wanted to introduce a new language into the program at the middle school and high school and we see this as an opportunity to introduce French.

-I would like to see us offer Japanese, because of the opportunities it would provide students, but as of right now we haven't found a teacher.

How do policymakers make informed decisions about which language to offer? Is the educator the one who knows best? Is the request of the parents the best option? How can issues around teacher availability be resolved so that other languages are more easily offered? There are several options to consider in choosing a language (or languages) for the program. Table 12 outlines some of these options.

Table 12

Options for Language Choice

Survey the community
Offer a lesser taught language (Arabic, Chinese, Japanese, Russian)
Offer a language new to the program
Offer several languages (spread over different elementary schools)
Offer different languages on a rotating entry basis
Offer multiple entry points into other languages (sixth grade, ninth grade, etc.)
Offer opportunity to study multiple languages at middle school or high school

Each option presents an opportunity and a challenge. The number of programs offering less commonly taught languages (i.e. Arabic, Chinese, Japanese, and Russian) is "remarkably small in light of the active discussions that take place in reports on educational reform regarding the need for a language-competent America" (Met, 1994, p. 155). Met explained,

> The discussions (of reform) have tended to focus on needs related to competition for global markets and diplomacy. Were foreign language course offerings and enrollments to reflect the priorities stated for expanded and improved foreign language instruction in the schools, we would expect to see substantially greater interest in courses in Chinese, Russian, Korean, Japanese, and others. Clearly, the

calls for improved language competence found in reports of educational reform are not reflected in what schools offer and what students take (Met, 1994, p. 155). Realities around teacher availability cannot be changed overnight. The wishes of the community cannot be ignored. The concerns of secondary teachers must be addressed. The opportunity to meet global realities must be considered.

All of the districts involved in this analysis selected Spanish as the language, except for one, which offers Chinese. Another district offers Russian to gifted students in the elementary schools. Most districts surveyed the community in order to choose the language. What are the implications of choosing one language (any language) over others? The FLES teachers interviewed were keenly aware of the anxiety caused by the choice of language on staff at the middle and high school levels. The concern is that offering one language will cause attrition in the other languages. Will the other languages suffer if Spanish is the prevailing choice for FLES programs? One administrator states,

> We found it to be a real struggle, and it still is, to deal with the choice of language. On one hand, Spanish makes sense for us. It is all around us and there are more and more Hispanics living in our communities. On the other hand, our staff (at the middle school and high school) works so hard, they are great teachers, but I can't assure them that they will not have to worry for their jobs. I am not sure what will happen myself.

An administrator from another state was interviewed about this issue. She related her situation,

We have had Spanish from Kindergarten to sixth grade now. I can tell you that

the other languages (French and Italian) have seen increases. We take a proactive

stance with these languages. (The teachers) go to the fifth grade classes with

videos, presentations with kids, a great publicity effort, and I think this makes a

difference. Kids see these languages as nice options. They go in right before the

kids make a choice about continuing or choosing another language at the middle

school. If we get proactive about it, we can ensure the maintenance of the other

languages.

There are two approaches to addressing the choice of language question:

consulting research or reviewing current practice. If we look to research to try to answer

this question, there is only one study that addresses the effect of language choice in FLES

programs on enrollment at the secondary level (Watzke & Grundstad, 1996). The

findings indicate a positive relationship between the language offered at an early age and

the language chosen at the secondary level. While the implication may be study in a

particular language at the elementary school may impact negatively on other languages

offered, the authors stated,

> The intention of this study was not to identify causal associations, but rather, to
>
> identify issues associated with student choice…Conclusions suggesting causality
>
> of various forms of early language study and student choice are beyond the scope
>
> of this study and require more sophisticated data collection and analysis methods
>
> (p. 22).

The second approach is to examine what actually happens in practice in school

districts with FLES programs. Most of the programs have not been in existence long enough to analyze impact at this time. In three of the FLES programs studied on Long Island, the enrollment in French and Italian rose with the first year of Spanish FLES students entering the middle school. Again, there may be many other variables that influenced this outcome. Future research is needed to examine the effect of language choice on enrollment in other languages at the secondary level.

In summary, language choice brings up several issues that need consideration by the FLES committee. A first position could be that there is no one best language to choose. Following this logic, the language chosen as best for the individual school district by the FLES committee is best for that district. This decision may be based on the characteristics of the community, projections of population trends, or other data. A second position would be that if the purpose of second language study were to foster global competitiveness, the study of certain languages (e.g. lesser-taught languages) may serve this purpose better than other languages. A third position would be to base language choice on the availability of qualified teachers. A final position would be to base language choice on the concern over negative effects on the secondary level. This must be weighed against the reality for each school district. Since research is not currently available to support or reject this final concern, each district should conduct its own action research to assess the effect of language choice for FLES on the total language program.

Districts can become proactive about maintaining enrollment in other languages through publicity and by offering multiple entry points into the other languages taught. Some school districts in other states have offered FLES programs in the languages already offered at the secondary level with the weakest enrollment to enhance enrollment in that language.

Spiraling up from K or down from 6. The decision about where to begin instruction in a K-12 program may seem simple. Most programs start at Kindergarten and spiral up in to the higher grades. Several of the districts on Long Island found this to be problematic, mostly because of the popularity and success of the program. Parents of the first through fifth-grade students were upset that their children had not been able to participate since the program started with Kindergarten. In order to deal with the concern of the parents, three of the districts offered a supplementary program to the students in other grade levels. For example, in one district, students in grades two through five are given mini-semesters in the language. In another district, they decided to bring the FLES program into all grade levels after the first year of implementation. In another district, they are offering after school and Saturday programs for the other grade levels. These attempts were made during the start-up years so that students who were not able to participate (e.g. they were in grades one-five and the program started with Kindergarten students the first year) were given access to the program, even on a limited basis.

Cost Analysis and Funding. Funding is another obstacle or challenge to implementing a FLES program. School boards must approve a new budget line with expenses for the program. Most districts built the program on funds from the local school district budget. Several districts began the program with a small start-up grant from a Federal agency. Other districts applied for and received a grant from the United States Department of

Education to incorporate technology in the FLES program. Comments from two of the FLES teachers interviewed relate to budget issues:

-Once we got the program going, the money was not a concern anymore.

-When we cut back the program because of budget cutbacks, the parents got so angry, went to board meetings, and complained, and then we got our funds back. I couldn't believe it, but it felt great.

Table 13 is a representation of a start-up cost analysis for a FLES program. This analysis is based on data shared from the interviews of the school districts on Long Island and the FLES Report written by Lawrence Public Schools (see Appendix O, see also a template prepared by Mimi Met in Rosenbusch, 1991, p. 312).

The cost of a program will vary with the size of the district, the experience of the teachers hired, the amount of instructional time planned, and allowances for curriculum development, materials, staff development, and supplies. The teacher's salary is the biggest expense of the program. The most cost-effective way of implementing a FLES program is by hiring elementary school teachers who already have secondary certification in a foreign language. These teachers can then obtain the extension for teaching a language other than English at the elementary school level. Instead of scheduling a "push in" to teach the classes, and paying an additional salary, this teacher becomes the "in-class" FLES teacher.

Where is this money going to be found? How can school districts justify this additional expense especially in districts with smaller budgets? While funding for a FLES program is drawn from the school or district budget, there are federal funds available to help state and local educational agencies establish and improve foreign language instruction in elementary and secondary schools. Table 13 provides an analysis of the

start-up costs of a FLES program.

Table 13

Cost Analysis for Starting a FLES Program on Long Island

Expense Category:	Projection/Related Information:
Teacher Salary (Most starting salaries for teachers on Long Island are approximately $40,000. Years of experience would increase the salary).	Approximately 1 teacher per 200 Students
Benefits	Negotiated in contract, roughly 20-25% of salary
Certification/Training	$650.00 course fees and textbooks through Dowling Institute (1999)
Staff Development	5 Conference Days annually at approximately $100 per day (this category will vary)
Curriculum Development	15 days for two teachers for first three years (most FLES teachers stated this as time needed to develop curriculum)
Instructional Materials	The districts surveyed showed ranges from $200 - $15,000, depending on district size and budget agreements
Supplies	The district surveyed showed ranges from $100 - $6,000, depending on district size and budget agreements

In 1998, $5 million dollars was targeted through the United States Department of

Education's Foreign Language Assistance Program (FLAP). The Department also

supports development of innovative educational projects and advanced teacher training

through other grants and projects" (Boston, 1998, p. 42). As of December 1999, $2

million dollars was available as grant money through this program (United States

Department of Education, 1999, personal communication with officer). In 2000, the

amount available will be $ 8,000,000 (Learning Languages, 1999, p. 21). A listing of these projects and agencies is provided in Appendix H. It is hoped that this amount will continue to rise in future years.

Table 14 is a sample of a cost breakdown for a district with 5 elementary schools (200 students in each school). The model assumes 30 minutes daily of foreign language instruction per pupil, with a "push-in" model. Costs will obviously vary from district to district depending on the number of elementary schools, the number of students, and other features of the program.

Table 14

Cost Breakdown for First Four Years of a FLES Program

Cost (Based on 5 Teachers) approximately 1 teacher per 200 students:	Explanation of Cost:
5 Teachers = $240,000	Expecting several teachers with several years of experience, and several teachers with no experience
Benefits = $55,000	Estimation of standard contract benefits
Certification = $3,250	$650.00 course fees and textbooks through Dowling Institute (1999)
Staff Development = $2,500	5 Conference Days annually at approximately $100 per day, per teacher
Curriculum Development = $1,875 ($ 625 after 3 years)	15 days per teacher for first three years (two teachers, estimating 5 hours per day at approximately $25.00 p/h)
Instructional Materials = $7,500 ($1,500 per building) ($ 800 per building after 3 years)	Most purchasing will occur during first three years. Including carts, books, puppets, software, maps, cassettes, videos, charts, games, flashcards, transparencies, flags, clocks, magazines, sentence holders, etc.
Supplies = $4,000 ($800 per building)	Including paper, markers, poster board, felt, stickers, coloring books from other countries, food items, glue, tape, etc.
Cost Year 1: $314,125 Cost Year 2: $310,875 Cost Year 3: $310,875 Cost Year 4: $306,125	After completion of certification, curriculum development, and acquisition of instructional materials, costs will drop

Summary

The obstacles to implementing a FLES program mentioned most frequently by people from Long Island school districts were finding time in the school day and the cost or funding. The discussion in this section shows there are various ways to find time in the school day, without negatively affecting performance in other subject areas. A district's level of commitment to developing cross cultural acceptance and language proficiency will help determine the amount of expense it is willing to incur to gain the benefits of a FLES program.

Section Nine

Political and Social Issues

The discussion of political and social issues relative to early second language

programs may revolve around multicultural education and issues of equity. The literature

and research in these areas shows a logical connection between the theories and goals for

second language education, multicultural education, and social issues of equal access.

The connection between second language programs and multicultural education

has not been explored extensively. These two fields often have a parallel goal, the

development of intercultural acceptance. Research in each of these areas has not

examined the connections of these programs and the paradigms that underlie their

instructional frameworks with one another.

Multicultural education may be defined in many terms (Banks, 1991b, 1994;

Goldberg, 1994). Banks (1991b) explained that "multicultural education requires that the

total school environment be restructured and transformed to reflect the racial and cultural

diversity within American society and to help children from diverse groups experience

educational equality" (p. 246). In his model of the multicultural school environment, two

of the eight conceptual frameworks are: "(1) The school has norms and values that

reflect and legitimize ethnic and cultural diversity, and (2) Language pluralism and

diversity are valued and fostered in the school" (Banks & Lynch, 1986, p. 23). Second

language instruction may be viewed as one of the components in this instructional

paradigm. In particular, second language programs that include a comprehensive

approach to developing cultural proficiency attend to these multicultural issues (Tedick &

Walker, 1996). "Students learning culture as process, for example, engage in cross-cultural comparisons and analyses, explore values and beliefs, and examine stereotypes and culturally-conditioned behavior" (Ramirez, 1998, p. 327).

In a discussion of multiculturalism and equity issues, Trugly and Garcia (1998) stated the relevance of early second language instruction to these issues,

It is not always the case that foreign language programs provide leadership in the area of national and international multiculturalism. It must be so at the elementary level, however. The staff must recognize that their duties require working with children at all skill levels and of all socioeconomic and racial/ethnic backgrounds...We must strive to plan to deliver a curriculum that is purposely and purposefully inclusive (p. 220).

A low socioeconomic background may put a child in the "at-risk" category for success in school (Wehlage & Rutter, 1986). These children are able to succeed in foreign language classes through the instructional techniques that are known to support them, such as cooperative learning. Holobow (1987) shared data that indicate students from low socioeconomic backgrounds and diverse abilities were able to perform as well as other groups in their French immersion classes. Heining-Boynton (1994) discussed the congruence of the instructional needs of these children and the communicative approach to foreign language instruction. Documentation of a successful learning experience for "at-risk" children in foreign language classes in New York City is shared by Spinelli (1996, pp. 72-3).

Holobow et al. (1987, 1991) reported on a series of studies of the achievement of low socioeconomic groups and diverse ethnic and racial groups in immersion programs. The findings indicated, "socioeconomically underprivileged children (both black and white) benefited from an immersion-type introduction to a foreign language as much as pupils from middle class homes" (Holobow et al., 1987, p. 137). In addition, "it was found that the working class black students scored as well as the middle class and white students on the French language tests" (Holobow et al., 1991, p. 179). Caldas and Boudreaux (1999) examined "whether being educated in an immersion program contributes or detracts from the academic performance of low socioeconomic status (SES) children" (p. 4). Their findings indicated these students do significantly better on standardized tests in English language arts and math than non-immersion students. While these studies focus on immersion, their implications are important for all second language programs.

In the statement of philosophy for the National Standards for Foreign Language Learning (1996), it is stated, "All students can be successful language and culture learners, and they must have access to language and culture study that is integrated into the entire school experience" (p. 7). As we support second language learning for ALL children, we are also supporting the development of cultural awareness, acceptance, and academic success for ALL children.

Section Ten

Beginning the Process of Implementation

The first step in initiating a FLES program is to establish a committee (see Section Fifteen, Table 19). Once the "FLES committee" has established a timeframe for meeting, reviewed the literature on FLES, and visited other programs, the committee should be ready to write a proposal for beginning world languages at the elementary school level. This proposal may include the following items:

- A Statement of Philosophy
- A Rationale for the Program (citing research)
- Program Goals
- A Description of the Model Chosen (schedules, grades, etc.)
- Cost Analysis (staffing, staff development, materials, supplies, etc.)
- Curriculum and Materials
- Community Involvement
- Assessment and Evaluation
- Bibliography

It is important that each committee member contribute to the process. One approach might be to assign each section of the proposal to a committee member. That person would read the literature related to that topic and write that section of the proposal. The sections are interrelated, which implies that a constant dialogue is necessary during the writing process. The major components of the program must be decided upon before proceeding to the other sections. For example, the description or design of the model must be discussed before attempting a cost analysis.

The following is a discussion of each section of the proposal. At the end of this discussion, a worksheet is provided for writing a proposal. Additional information for each section can be found earlier in this document in Sections Three, Four, Six, and Eight.

Statement of Philosophy. In this section, the committee members will discuss their commitment to providing a global education to children in our schools. The National and State Standards should be mentioned as part of the conceptual framework for the proposal.

Rationale for a FLES Program. The rationale for a program describes the purpose(s) of the program. As mentioned in Section Three of this book, the rationale for a FLES program is based on developing cultural sensitivity and enhanced language learning skills. A statement of the benefits or outcomes found in research-based studies should be cited. Below are two examples:

➢ Students who study a world language at the elementary level may have greater sensitivity towards others (Carpenter & Torney, 1974; Rhodes, et. al, 1989; Riestra & Johnson, 1964).

➢ Students who study a world language at the elementary level may have increased proficiency in the language due to longer exposure (ACTFL, 1999; Brega & Newell, 1967; Corbin & Chiachere, 1997; Curtain, 1993; Curtain & Pesola, 1994; Donato, et al., 1996; Dulay, Burt, & Krashen, 1982; Harley, 1998; Krashen, Scarcella, & Long, 1982; Lipton, Morgan, & Reed, 1996; Long, 1990; Vocolo, 1967; Vollmer, 1962).

Additional benefits (such as enhanced creative and divergent thinking, higher scores on standardized tests, etc.) should be mentioned in this section. Well-developed concepts supported by leaders in the field should also be mentioned in this section. Below are several examples:

➢ Studying a world language at the elementary level may enhance cognitive skills, such as creative and divergent thinking (Foster & Reeves, 1989; Landry, 1973; 1974).

➢ Students who study a world language at the elementary level may have improved scores on standardized tests, such as the SATs (Cooper, 1987; Eddy, 1981; The College Board, 1992).

➢ Students who study a world language may improve their knowledge of their own language (Curtain, 1992; National Standards for Foreign Language Learning, 1995; Vygostky, 1984).

Program Goals. The specific goals of the program for the specific school district should be mentioned. If the district has a mission statement, connection to this statement should be made. In addition, opportunities for reinforcement of elementary curriculum should be discussed.

A Description of the Model Chosen. In this section, the committee should give details of the model chosen (schedules, grades, etc.). The distinction between a FLEX and FLES model should be made clear and the reasons for the model chosen should be given.

Cost Analysis. The preparation of a cost analysis should reflect the design or model selected. A general guideline may be established to estimate the number of teachers needed. A building with 200 students, meeting with a FLES teacher daily for thirty minutes should require one teacher (see Met in Rosenbusch, 1991). In addition, the district should plan for the cost of materials, supplies, video, cassettes, computer software, and travel carts. While staff development and curriculum writing are part of the start up costs, a plan for continuing staff development should be in place. If the district plans to initiate a "phase-in" of the program over several years, special sessions offered to other grades may likely become an issue. Planning for additional stipends or other resources to support learning for the "non-phase-in" grade levels should be considered.

Curriculum and Materials. Most districts use "teacher-prepared" curriculum and materials. It is important that the FLES teacher is given the opportunity to write curriculum plans for the program. This is usually done during the summer months before the program is started. The best content-related curriculum and materials are prepared with the assistance of the classroom teacher. Establishing a team (of the FLES teacher and the classroom teacher) for curriculum writing will ensure the greatest success for this type of program. The market has increased the availability of folk literature, songs, videos, puppets, and other specific materials geared towards FLES programs. The cost of these items will depend on preferences and number of teachers, but each teacher should be equipped with a cart, puppets, the prepared curriculum written with the classroom teacher, and other materials researched and deemed appropriate.

Community Involvement. From the inception of the FLES committee, parents should be involved in and aware of the FLES program. They can be the greatest advocates and support systems. Once the program is established, parents can be kept informed of the content, events, and successes of the program through a monthly Newsletter (see sample in Appendix L). Parents and members of the community can be invited into the FLES classes, special programs, assemblies, etc. to offer their expertise, chaperone, or assist. The National Standard for Foreign Languages, number five (Communities), states that students should "use the language within and beyond the school setting," and for "personal enjoyment and enrichment" (Standards for Foreign Language Learning, 1996,

p. 9). A wonderful opportunity for publicity, enrichment, and attainment of this standard

is through participation in contests and competitions sponsored by professional

organizations of foreign language teachers. FLES teachers should be encouraged to

enroll students in these types of events. Many local chapters of AATs (American

Association of Teachers of World Languages) offer competitions and enrichment

activities, in addition to state and local organizations (see listing of professional

organizations in Appendix M).

Assessment and Evaluation. The desire for data based on many forms of assessment has

swept the nation. While students in FLES programs can be assessed to determine levels

of achievement, it is important that these levels of achievement are based on several

concepts:

1. The goals specific to the program and the district

2. The design and model of the program

3. The understanding that second language development at the elementary level is not

    reading and writing intensive

4. The results of assessment measures should be used to enhance the program, not to

    penalize the students

5. The best methods of assessment are developed locally, by the FLES teacher, since

    s/he is aware of the learning process experienced by the children

6.   Assessment should not be given in one format, but rather in various formats so that

    all children are able to demonstrate learning (i.e. authentic assessment, multiple

    intelligence, etc.)

Assessment of student achievement may be one part of program evaluation. Specific surveys or instruments can be used to provide data on the program (see sample program evaluation instruments in Appendix K and Section Fourteen). The feedback from students, FLES teachers, classroom teachers, parents, and administrators is necessary to provide a strong program.

Bibliography. A comprehensive bibliography of all pertinent literature should be compiled. The bibliography should also include websites viewed and curriculum resources examined.

Two additional sections may be added to the proposal: Reflection on Committee Process and Impact Analysis. These sections provide the opportunity for a dialogue between the audience to the proposal and the committee members.

Reflection on Committee Process. At several stages of engagement of the FLES committee, it is useful to allow for reflection on the process. This can be accomplished through minutes at meetings, journals, videotaping, summaries of activities, and reports of subcommittees. Some items that may be included in this section are the schools visited, the frequently asked questions, the items to be addressed later on in the process, and any other phase of implementation. This information may be shared with members of the Board of Education (see Section Eleven for a discussion of Board presentations), or district employees who might be interested in understanding the process.

Impact Analysis. Members of the committee should examine and provide a summary of the extent of the impact on the program. This section will also reflect specific needs, concerns, or obstacles the district faces in implementing a FLES program. Recommendations for meeting these obstacles should be addressed.

FLES Proposal Worksheet:

- **Statement of Philosophy**

_____
_____
_____
_____
_____
_____
_____

- **Rationale for the Program (citing research)**

_____
_____
_____
_____
_____
_____
_____

- **Program Goals**

_____
_____
_____
_____
_____
_____
_____

- **Description of the Model Chosen (schedules, grades, etc.)**

_____
_____
_____
_____
_____
_____

- **Cost Analysis (staffing, staff development, materials, supplies, etc.)**

_____
_____
_____
_____
_____
_____

- **Curriculum and Materials**

  _____
  _____
  _____
  _____
  _____
  _____
  _____

- **Community Involvement**

  _____
  _____
  _____
  _____
  _____
  _____
  _____

- **Assessment and Evaluation**

  _____
  _____
  _____
  _____
  _____
  _____
  _____

Section Eleven

Presenting to the Board of Education

After drafting a proposal, the committee can present the proposal to the Board of Education. Representatives from the committee can highlight the most important information from each section. The proposal can be summarized into one attractive page. The committee should also prepare a list of "Frequently Asked Questions" to help address the most common concerns (see Table 15). A very effective presentation also includes visuals such as photos or videotapes. (An example of a news broadcast dealing with the "critical window" for language learning is available from NBC's Dateline series, Catalogue # NDL971128).

Table 15

Frequently Asked Questions

Frequently Asked Questions
What does the research say about early language learning?
What methodologies would be best?
What are the goals of the program?
Does the classroom teacher need to have second language skills?
How will we fit this into the school day?
Who will teach the classes?
How will learning another language affect the learning of English?
How do we incorporate the regular elementary curriculum onto the FLES program?
Should children with special needs be included in the program?
Which language should we select?
What will happen to other languages offered in the middle/junior or high school?
How will we staff the program?
Where will we get the funds?
What happens when a child comes into the district and has missed several years of the language program?
How will we assess the students' learning?

Section Twelve

The Elementary World Language Student

A well-designed FLES program attends to the developmental interests and needs of the students. Children at each grade level have unique learning experiences and learning styles. It is imperative that the FLES teacher collaborates with the classroom teacher to integrate curriculum and to understand the learning process for various learning and developmental stages throughout the elementary years.

FLES teachers must be familiar with the theories of child development. Heining-Boynton (1991) categorizes the developmental stages of the elementary-aged child using the theoretical frameworks of Piaget (1959), Behler & Snowman (1986), and Bredekamp (1986). The learning stages are divided into three age-related groups: Preschool and Kindergarten, Early Primary Grades (1-3), and Later Primary Grades (4-6). These stages are sub-divided, in his discussion, to analyze four domains of experience (physical, cognitive, social, and emotional). He states that, "attention to these characteristics of development will assist…in planning and delivering materials and will become an integral part of…[the FLES] methodology" (p. 4).

Heining-Boynton reminds us that children do not fit neatly into these categories. In addition, Piaget's theories have been critiqued by child psychologists (Toulmin, 1972), yet the essence of this discussion is to highlight the importance of attending to the differences in abilities, interests, and learning styles of young children. Table 16 summarizes the major points in Heining-Boynton's article.

Table 16

Developmental Comparison of Elementary Aged Children (Heining-Boynton, 1991)

The Preschool and Kindergarten Child (preoperational, ages 2-6)	
Physical Domain	active learners, clumsy, poor eye-hand coordination, energy bursts and drops, visual acuity is a problem, large muscle development, great flexibility, enjoy showing off
Cognitive Domain	time for language development, eager to learn, uninhibited, play with language, make up their own rules, numerous errors, generalize rules, learn from hearing correct model, not by repeating individual corrections, self-correct, need concrete examples, direct interaction with material needed
Social Domain	very social, less inhibited than older children, willing to Participate in a wide range of activities, relate to cultural Similarities, enjoy dramatic play, respond to concrete Examples relating to their own experiences, friends change rapidly, frequent and short quarrels with peers, parallel play, not good at cooperative learning
Emotional Domain	adults are very important, excited about learning, influenced very easily, model attitudes and behaviors of adults, sensitive to correction, vulnerable, easily hurt, may cry easily, outbursts of anger and temper tantrums possible, jealous of peers, seek a lot of attention

The Early Primary Grades 1-3 (concrete operational, ages 7-9)	
Physical Domain	activity very important, fatigue easily, fine motor skills problems (especially for boys), eye-hand coordination problems in writing and reading, use big manipulatives, large print books, children overestimate their physical abilities, can easily get carried away with work/activity
Cognitive Domain	eager learners, more competent in verbal skills, concrete learning with a large variety of sensor input, use many examples
Social Domain	socially oriented, friendship patterns less flexible, developing permanent friends, more selective in choices, quarrels may be frequent, good management required, rule-bound games can be problematic, avoid games with losers, avoid pitting girls against boys,
Emotional Domain	becoming sensitive to the feelings of others, increased level of cultural awareness, draw parallels to their own culture to maintain concreteness of examples, very sensitive to ridicule, criticism, and failure, refrain from asking a child to repeat correct answer, model for the class and ask for choral repetition instead, offer gentle and sensitive correction

The Later Primary Grades 4-6 (concrete operational-formal operational, ages 9-12)	
Physical Domain	significant physical changes, growth spurt, especially for girls, social awkwardness, unwanted attention, physical discomforts, heightened concern over sex roles and sexuality, use boy/girl activities with discretion, fine motor coordination is excellent at this time, reading and writing skills advanced, sense of competence about reading and writing
Cognitive Domain	more aware of individual differences, learning styles more apparent, abstract thinking apparent, most children still rely on generalizations from concrete examples, expect higher-order examples and problems, cause and effect analyzed
Social Domain	peers begin to replace adults in importance, eagerness to learn dissipates
Emotional Domain	behavior disorders peak by sixth grade, boys often seen as more difficult than girls at this age, tendency is to give boys more attention, students feel caught between adult and peer pressures, students are afraid of failure, channel attention seeking behaviors into active participation

The implications of these categories are: (1) FLES teachers should be informed in the areas of child development, (2) the world language curriculum should be meaningful and age-appropriate, and (3) FLES teachers should be able to interact with classroom teachers and other building specialists to provide the most enriching experiences for all students.

Below is a list of approaches and activities for elementary students. FLES teachers from across the nation have shared these and many other ideas through a listserv created for FLES teachers, Ñandu (see Appendix M for steps to join). Details, resources, and specifics instructions for activities can be found in the Ñandu archives. Curtain and Pesola (1992) and Lipton (1998) share and explain a plethora of ideas, approaches and activities. Teachers planning curriculum for a FLES program might examine available materials, observe other teachers, and experiment with a variety of techniques to create appropriate activities. The activities listed can be used with children at any age level.

Content-Related Approach Magic Box Puppets
Standards Approach Fantasy Trips Learning Centers
Cultural Approach Charades Paired Activities
Thematic Approach White Boards Felt/Flannel Boards
Songs/Music Fly Swatters Word Wall
Cooperative Learning Language Ladders Password Expressions
Graphic Organizers Shower Curtain Displays Gouin Series - *like TPRS*
DBQs Big Books Packing a Suitcase
Charts/Graphs Math Manipulatives ESP Game
Menus/Meal taking Mathematic Equations Brainstorming
Literature/Folktales Science Experiments Round Robin Games
Nursery Rhymes Does it Float or Sink? Dialogues/Role Play
Webbing Cinquains/Concrete Poems Realia
Venn Diagrams Simon Says Chants
Email to epals Book Making Guessing Games
Internet/WebQuests Making Crafts Computer Programs

A Sample Activity for Pre-K Children:

_____
_____
_____
_____
_____
_____
_____

A Sample Activity for Early Primary Children:

_____
_____
_____
_____
_____
_____
_____

A Sample Activity for Late Primary Children:

_____
_____
_____
_____
_____
_____
_____

Some FLES teachers have made the transition from the secondary student to the elementary-aged student. Most teachers feel especially rewarded through this experience. Some of these educators may not have spent many hours working with young children. In preparation, it is a good idea to observe elementary classes and children, in addition to reading literature, and reflecting on one's own knowledge base. One method of practicing this reflects is to write a profile of an "imaginary child." A FLES teacher should be able to describe what a child is like, what s/he likes to do, how s/he behaves in class, etc. The teacher can create a "progression" of what this child may be like at the middle school and finally the high school.

A Profile of an Elementary-Aged Child

_____

_____

_____

_____

_____

_____

The Child at the Middle School

_____

_____

_____

_____

_____

_____

The Child at the High School

_____

_____

_____

_____

_____

_____

Section Thirteen

Writing the Curriculum

The Ideal FLES Curriculum is one that is based on the content from the
elementary curriculum. Despite some fears or concerns that FLES teachers may not have
mastery of content, many FLES teachers enthusiastically support the concept that
children can learn, review, and relearn content from other subject areas through the target
language. The most important issues to consider in the process of devising a content-
related curriculum are summarized in an article by Curtain & Haas (1995). They state:

(1) Become familiar with the regular classroom curriculum by
   observing…reading the school's curriculum guide…talking with teachers
   about their curriculum and to the students about what they are studying.

(2) Plan to integrate content that you are interested in and will take time to
   research. Start on a small scale and select only one or two topics…

(3) Use a web or a curriculum planning format that promotes the integration of
   language, content, and culture.

(4) Design interesting activities for the students that use prior knowledge and
   personal experience, work in a variety of groupings…challenge the
   students…and address the students' multiple ways of learning (p. 2).

Research has shown that meaningful and engaging material is more likely
to be retained in long term memory (Krashen, 1981). Including content from the
elementary curriculum provides children with meaningful leaning experiences. They are
able to build on prior knowledge as they use the language in the new context (Brinton,
Snow, & Wesche, 1989). A content-based curriculum is part of a strong, well-defined

FLES program. An example of a content-related unit, based on the Boynton's stages of child development, is presented below.

Integrating language study with a unit on Safety. A class of Pre-K students is shown the three colors of a traffic light. The students repeat the colors as they receive three circles, one of each color. Students pass the colors to each other, naming the colors. The students repeat and act out the words for "stop/slow down/go" in the target language as they hold up and name each color. Large colored hoops are placed on the floor. Students jump from one hoop to the other, naming the colors. Students color in a picture of a traffic sign as they sing a song about safety using the three colors.

A class of early primary students counts the number of traffic lights shown in a representation of a city or town. They graph the number of each color on a chart. Students make signs with paper plates and colored paper. They copy the words for stop/slow down/go onto the signs. Students are shown drawings of different scenes in a town. They hold up the signs suited for each situation. Students play a TPR game (red light, green light one, two, three) in the target language.

A class of late primary students is shown a video clip or an overhead depicting a conversation between two people about traveling safely. The teacher models the conversation. Asking questions and using gestures, the teacher models the responses for cross at the green, etc. Students are shown traffic signs from the target culture. In pairs, the students match the signs with the appropriate expressions. Using the new expressions, the teacher asks students to fill in missing parts of a conversation. Pairs act out the conversation. Students sing a song about safety.

Content-related curriculum for the FLES program can be prepared during summer curriculum work as a joint effort of the FLES teacher and the classroom teacher. Mapping themes across grade levels will assist the FLES teacher in defining topics of entry for the curriculum. A sample map is presented below (not all subject areas are included).

Table 17

Mapping Content with FLES

Grade	MATH	SCIENCE	HEALTH	GLOBAL STUDIES	LANGUAGE ARTS
Kindergarten					
First					
Second					
Third					
Fourth					
Fifth					

Several lesson plans created by FLES teachers are shared in Appendix N. The teachers have included culture, creativity, engaging activities, content, and age/developmentally appropriate activities in their work.

Section Fourteen

A Final Word on Assessment and Program Evaluation

One of the most important pieces to a strong and well-developed FLES program is the program evaluation component. The FPEI (FLES Program Evaluation Instrument, see Appendix K) is a very accessible and adaptable tool for program assessment. This survey (prepared by Heining-Boynton, 1991) provides an opportunity to gain feedback and insights into the successes and weaknesses of the program.

Assessment of student performance may also be a component in program evaluation. Student assessment can be done on an individual basis, or through an examination of a representative sample of students. It is possible to obtain a sense of student achievement in the language without taking the extensive amount of time that would be necessary to test each child. By taking a random sample of an appropriate number of students from each elementary school (at least 25 students) and asking them questions, the coordinator of the world language program may be able to ascertain the progress towards the goals of the program.

The purpose of the evaluation would be threefold: (1) to assess student achievement in the language, (2) to assess the cultural awareness of the students, and (3) to obtain feedback on attitudes towards the program. Using this type of evaluation (direct contact with a limited number of students), the coordinator might ask the FLES teachers to compile a list of 10-12 questions that the students should be able to answer. The coordinator meets with the students and in a casual, game-like setting as she interviews the students. A representation of this type of report is presented below.

A Sample FLES Program Evaluation and Student Assessment Instrument

Name_____

Language_____

School_____

<u>Please list ten questions in the target language that you believe the elementary students will be able to ask and/or answer:</u>

1-_____

2-_____

3-_____

4-_____

5-_____

6-_____

7-_____

8-_____

9-_____

10-_____

Data could be compiled in a format similar to the one below, where the administrator marks a check for each correct answer given by each student. The administrator could also record responses to questions about attitude and cultural awareness.

<u>Elementary Foreign Language Program—Student Assessment</u>

School _____ Language _____

Questions:	Student:	1	2	3	4	5	6	7	8	9	10
1- ?											
2- ?											
3- ?											
4- ?											
5- ?											
6- ?											
7- ?											
8- ?											
9- ?											
10-?											

School _____ Language _____

Questions:	Student:	1	2	3	4	5	6	7	8	9	10
1- ?											
2- ?											
3- ?											
4- ?											
5- ?											
6- ?											
7- ?											
8- ?											
9- ?											
10-?											

School _____ Language _____

Questions:	Student:	1	2	3	4	5	6	7	8	9	10
1- ?											
2- ?											
3- ?											
4- ?											
5- ?											
6- ?											
7- ?											
8- ?											
9- ?											
10-?											

To:

From:

Re: Evaluation of FLES Program

Date:

As per arrangements with the elementary schools, an evaluation was conducted of

the FLES program with the purpose of determining the following:

1-the second language ability of the students,

2-the cultural awareness attained,

3-the opinions held by the students about the program.

The principals and/or the world language teacher randomly selected ten children

from each of the elementary schools. The students were evenly distributed among grade

levels. The gender of the students was 50% boys and 50% girls. Attached is a summary

of the rate of accuracy of their responses (based on percentage of questions answered

correctly out of the total number asked). An anecdotal summary of the songs and

opinions about the program is also included.

Also attached is a record of the questions and answers. The check marks indicate

an appropriate response. An "X" indicates an inability to respond. If the space is blank,

the question was not asked for that student. After the interview, students were asked to

sing songs they knew in the target language and talk about "what else they learned."

They were also asked questions in English about how they felt about the program.

I. <u>Summary of responses for interview:</u>

Accuracy Rate of Building	Accuracy Rate 67% or better	Accuracy Rate of 33%-66%	below 33%

II. <u>Songs and Cultural discussion:</u>

III. <u>Attitudes about the program:</u>

IV. <u>These are some of their comments:</u>

Several districts have attempted to include an evaluation of each individual student. While this is much more time and labor intensive, it might give more detailed information to the FLES teacher and the supervisor of the program. The most important point of reflection on attempting this process is to evaluate what will be done with the information obtained. Will students receive a grade? Will the program be cut back if expectations are not being met? Will the teachers and administrators re-evaluate their goals and expectations of the program?

The Center for Applied Linguistics has compiled a bank of assessments for K-8 world language programs (Thompson, 1995). The best assessment for any FLES program is one that is reflective of the various forms of assessment as well as the goals of the program, and most importantly, has a positive impact on the program, its teachers, and the children.

Section Fifteen

Summary and Conclusions

Summary of the Rationale for a FLES Policy

Why should a school district consider this policy? The first step in the implementation process is answering this question, Why should we implement this policy? The committee members must believe there is something in this policy that cannot be found in other policies or programs competing for time in the school day. The arguments presented by Curtain and Pesola (1994) address these issues.

Beginning foreign languages at the elementary school level *increases time practice and experience with the target language*, making possible a *much higher level of proficiency*. *Global awareness* and *sensitivity to others* are best developed in young children (Lambert & Klineberg, 1967). If we believe these skills are important components of our educational system, they should be introduced at the elementary level, along side of math, science, social studies, art, health, etc. (Curtain & Pesola, 1994, pp. 3-4).

The additional educational benefits for all children such *as increased academic achievement in other subject areas* (Armstrong & Rogers, 1997; Rafferty, 1986), higher performance on standardized tests such as the SAT test (Cooper, 1987; Eddy, 1981), and *enhanced creative and divergent thinking* (Foster & Reeves, 1989; Landry, 1974), only add to the rationale for early second language study.

Some school districts are combining foreign language study with other specials (art, music, and technology) to address the issue of competing programs. Students in one of the FLES programs on Long Island learn the target language as they work with computers, begin work in their art class, or warm up for physical education.

The FLES teachers interviewed stressed the importance of *a long sequence of learning to attain the goals for second language instruction*. A long sequence in second language may allow for more children to experience greater success with the language at the high school and post secondary levels. Successful, well-articulated FLES programs may give students the opportunity to *develop life-long second language learning skills*.

An educational argument for early second language study in Europe parallels many of the national, state, and local issues discussed in this document

The world has changed. Children meet members of other ethnic and speech communities more and more often and have to be prepared for these encounters. They need what we specialists call intercultural communicative competence fairly early. For this, they must acquire verbal skills in at least one other language and knowledge of other cultures. And if, as psychological and physiological findings tell us, they possess the necessary dispositions for the competence needed, then it is an educational obligation for educators to help them achieve such competence (Doyé & Hurrell, 1997, p. 12).

Table 18 provides a summary of the rationale and additional benefits of a FLES program.

Table 18

Summary of Rationale and Additional Benefits of FLES

Why have a FLES program?	Research, Related Literature, and Resources:
Increased proficiency in language due to longer exposure	American Council on the Teaching of Foreign Languages, 1999; Brega & Newell, 1967; Corbin & Chiachere, 1997; Curtain, 1993; Curtain & Pesola, 1994; Donato, et al., 1996; Dulay, Burt, & Krashen, 1982; Harley, 1998; Krashen, Scarcella, & Long, 1982; Lipton, Morgan, & Reed, 1996; Long, 1990; Vocolo, 1967; Vollmer, 1962
Greater sensitivity to speakers of other languages	Carpenter & Torney, 1974; Rhodes et al., 1989; Riestra & Johnson, 1964
Understanding and acceptance of other cultures	Carpenter & Torney, 1974; Rhodes et al., 1989; Riestra & Johnson, 1964
Creates positive attitude towards second language learning	Donato et al., 1996; Hancock et al., 1976
Multiculturalism and equity issues	Allport, 1954; Banks, 1991; Caldas & Boudreaux, 1999; Heining-Boynton, 1994; Holobow et. al, 1987, 1991; Slavin, 1995; Spinelli, 1996; Trugly & Garcia, 1998
Access to information and communications in a global world	Donato & Terry, 1995; Munks, 1996
Improved achievement in second language at HS level	Brega & Newell, 1967; Lipton, Morgan, & Reed, 1996; Mayuex, 1966; Vocolo, 1967; Vollmer, 1962
Give all students enhanced opportunity for success on NYS Regents Exam	Report of the New York State Foreign Language Implementation Committee, 1998
FLES students outperform other students in assessments of basic skills such as reading, language arts, and math	Armstrong & Rogers, 1997; Campbell, 1963; District of Columbia Public Schools, 1971; Garfinkel & Tabor, 1991; Johnson et al., 1961, 1963; Lopato, 1963; Nespor, 1970; Offenberg, 1971; Rafferty, 1986; Sheridan, 1976
Higher scores on SATs	College Board, 1992; Cooper, 1987; Eddy, 1981
Improve self-concept for all students, including the less-able and at-risk learner	Anadrade et. al, 1989; Genesee, 1976; Heining-Boynton, 1994; Masciantonio, 1977; Shrum, 1985; Spinelli, 1996
Greater divergent/creative thinking and enhanced cognitive skills	Foster & Reeves, 1989; Landry, 1973, 1974
Reinforcement of elementary curriculum	Crandall & Tucker, 1990; Curtain & Haas, 1995; Curtain & Pesola, 1994; Haas, 1999; Pesola, 1995; Lorenz & Met, 1990
Follow international, national, state-wide, and local trends	ACTFL, 1999; Branaman & Rhodes, 1997; Bergentoft, 1994; Margarita, 1999; New York State Association of Foreign Language Teachers, 1998; Rhodes & Oxford, 1988

<u>Summary of the Implementation Process</u>

If a school district endorses a policy of FLES, how should it be implemented? Implementation of foreign languages at the elementary school level requires changes in the school organization; changes in staffing, scheduling, materials, training, etc. It requires generating answers to the many questions posed in the previous sections.

If all the changes required for implementation of this new policy are to occur, the individuals involved, the teachers, the administrators, the parents, etc., must come to terms with the fact that organizations do not change on their own. A new policy cannot bring about the desired changes. It is the individuals, working together, listening to one another, putting aside assumptions, and moving forward in an open and participatory way, who make the changes possible (Osterman & Kottkamp, 1993).

One of the districts studied for this document created a "FLES Study team." These team members devoted many hours to researching, reading, sharing, deconstructing, and brainstorming through the process. One member said it was one of the best experiences she had in bringing about a change in the school system. Much of the success of the program lies in the strength and process of the committee.

School districts go through different planning and implementation processes. A synthesis of the steps taken and phases of implementation (provided in Table 19) clarifies what worked best for most districts and underscores the challenges encountered.

The work required of the FLES committee is intensive and demanding. The first product is a proposal for the policy. A sample proposal and report is presented in Appendix O. Each district must prepare a very individualized plan based on the district's community, needs, goals, mission statement, funding, and instructional programs.

Table 19   Summary of Implementation Process

Steps Taken:	Strategies and Considerations:
Form a planning committee	Include superintendent, principals, classroom teachers, FLES teachers, middle and high school foreign language teachers, parents, supervisor of foreign language department
Establish time frame for committee meetings and implementation	One year - one and ½ years
Review empirical/non-empirical literature	See References
Visit other programs	See Appendices A & B for Long Island Districts
Prepare a rationale and goals	See Sample Proposal (Appendix O)
Prepare a cost analysis	See Tables 13, 14 and Appendix O.
Decide how to fit the program into the school day	Some options are: Extend the length of the school day. Take 5-10 minutes from the core curricula areas. Use content-related instruction so time is considered reinforcement of curricula. Use foreign language in other specials (i.e. art, physical education…)
Choose where to start the program	Some options include: Begin at Kindergarten and spiral up. Spiral down from sixth grade. Push in at all grades. Begin at one grade and provide supplementary lessons to other grades.
Decide which language(s) will be taught	Some options include: Survey the community. Pick different languages for different buildings. Rotate languages on different entry years. Offer a lesser-taught language. Offer a new language to the district. Provide multiple entry opportunities for other languages (sixth grade, ninth grade, etc.).
Seek staff	Current secondary staff can obtain addendum. Current elementary staff with foreign language certification can obtain addendum. Advertise through FLTeach and Ñanduti (websites for foreign language teachers).
Devise an approach for integrating language, culture, and content areas	Based on National Standards: Communication, Cultures, Connections, Comparisons, Communities. Focus on integrating language, culture, and content through curriculum development, thematic planning, and materials.
Plan for curriculum writing for FLES teachers and classroom teachers	Allow for summer curriculum writing. Provide mutual planning time for FLES teacher and classroom teachers.
Provide opportunities for staff development and networking	See Appendices G & M.
Assess possible use of technology	Allow FLES teacher to meet with technology coordinator. Consider applying for grant money from federal agencies (see Appendix H).
Form a sub-committee to examine articulation issues	Members should include teachers from FLES program, junior high/middle school, high school, & program supervisor.
Devise a strategy for assessment of student progress	Portfolios, interviews, and other locally developed assessments, appropriate for the developmental stage of the children and based on program goals.
Devise a strategy for program evaluation	See Appendix K (FPEI, Heining-Boynton, 1991).
Plan to include ALL students	All students (special needs, at risk, etc.) should be included in the program.
Submit plans for public relations	See Section Six.

Summary of The Ideal FLES Model

What is the "Ideal Model" for a FLES program? This question was asked of the educators and administrators from districts with FLES programs, as well as leaders in the field. Combining these thoughts with data from research and discussion in the literature provided the framework for the Ideal Model.

The schedule for the Ideal Model is certainly a rigorous or intensive FLES schedule. Many districts are coming close to this ideal amount of exposure. Other districts may consider increasing time for the FLES class as the program evolves. Most districts have adopted a content-related approach. The curriculum written and materials purchased by these districts support learning of other subject areas (mainly language arts, science, and math).

Using content-related instruction as a framework for the FLES, balanced with language instruction and culture, may seem like a challenging task. Many of the FLES teachers interviewed shared their ideas and techniques for striking this balance through creativity and flexibility. This creativity is evident in their discussions about FLES and in their lesson plans (see Appendix N). Districts can enhance the existing program through the use of technology.

Finding a qualified and creative FLES teacher was expressed as a main concern. While most districts struggled with this issue at times, all existing programs have been staffed. As these programs continue to spiral into additional grades, they will seek new staff. Most of the administrators expressed great pleasure with the level of commitment, enthusiasm, knowledge base, and creativity of the FLES teachers hired.

Table 20

Summary of the Ideal FLES Model

Schedule	Instructional Approach	The FLES Teacher
K,1—5x a week, 15-20 minutes a day	Content-related curriculum (developed with classroom teacher)	Native/near-native proficiency in language
2,3—5x a week, 20-30 minutes a day	Encourages interaction among students, includes focus on language development	Well-versed in culture of target language
4,5—5x a week, 30-40 minutes a day	Class conducted primarily in target language	Very knowledgeable in developmental issues, interests, needs, and language-learning abilities of elementary-aged children
6—5x a week, 40 minutes a day	Includes technology when possible or appropriate	Has access to staff development and support networks (see Appendix M).

technology a challenge -push-

One of the weaknesses of the FLES programs from the 1960s was the lack of preparation of the teachers. Many people believed a FLES teacher need only have a small working knowledge of the language. The opposite is true. Since children will acquire speech sounds modeled, native-like accents serve the program best.

146

The language choice issue does not imply that only one language must be offered. School districts may be creative about which language(s) to offer and how. For example, in some states, school districts have successfully offered different languages to different elementary schools in the same district. A study of the languages most often selected by students in each building for previous enrollments may provide guidelines for this option. Other districts have rotated the languages or started languages on different entry years.

While scheduling more than one language in a given building is a near impossibility, it is very conceivable that students are offered multiple entry points into other languages. They may be encouraged to consider a new language through publicity at the time of entry into new languages. Several districts are offering alternative study programs for other languages (after school, on a Saturday, etc.). While this issue is a challenging one, creativity and cooperation will provide some solutions. The difficulties presented by this issue should not preclude a district from offering an early start for second language study all together.

Conclusion

The adoption and implementation of a foreign language policy at the elementary school level has increased in school districts nationwide and continues to gain the attention of the media (*Dateline*, 1997; *Newsday*, November 7, 1999). The trend to adopt a FLES policy may be a response to the context of the world in which we live. Learning other languages has become an international priority in many ways. "Simply put, the whole notion of 'foreign' language is growing increasing questionable, as changing demographic data indicate that American citizens now speak over a hundred and fifty languages in our cities, town, and neighborhoods" (Brecht & Walton, 1995). The terminology "world" language is certainly more accurate.

Accessing knowledge through language and culture will not be feasible in a short, limited sequence of second language learning. Offering the study of world languages at the elementary school level is the beginning of the acknowledgement that even a K-12 World Language Program is not enough. This document should be referring to a lifetime endeavor. The language learning process must continue past the school years, if it is to be truly successful. In their book, *Foreign language learning: The journey of a lifetime*, Donato and Terry stated, "Foreign languages are best learned through extended sequences of study beginning in the elementary school and continuing well into adulthood where conditions are created to use and be rewarded for using the foreign language" (p. v, 1995). It truly is a journey of a lifetime, and as the Chinese proverb says, a journey of a thousand miles, begins with one step.

Beginning the study of a second language in the elementary school is one step towards attaining the goals of: increased *time to practice and experience the target language, higher levels of proficiency in the target language, a long sequence of learning to attain the goals for second language instruction, life-long second language learning skills, increased academic achievement, increased creative and divergent thinking, enhanced self-concept, global citizenry, sensitivity towards others,* and *the peace that comes with harmony among diversity.*

Suggested Research

Throughout this document, it has been noted that additional research is needed to adequately understand FLES programs as well as the implications and effects they may have on many areas of education. Below is a list of future research possibilities that may add to the knowledge base currently available in the literature on FLES.

- Long-term and short-term studies of the effects of FLES programs on:

-second language proficiency (effect of age on achievement)

-attitudes towards people/languages of other cultures

-age and development of attitudes towards people/languages of other cultures

-performance in academic areas other than foreign languages

-performance on high stakes, standardized tests

- Long-term studies of the effects of language choice in a FLES program on other languages offered in the district

Whenever feasible, studies should use random samples of large numbers of students. Control and experimental groups should be equated for as many variables as possible.

References

Adcock, D. (1980). A comparison of the effects of three approaches upon the development of listening comprehension in Spanish and upon the improvement of reading skills in English of below-average readers enrolled in the first year of FLES Spanish (grade 4). (Doctoral Dissertation, Ohio State University, 1980). *Dissertation Abstracts International, 41-07A*, 2975.

Alkonis, N., & Brophy, M. (1961). A Survey of FLES Practices. *Reports of surveys and studies in the teaching of modern foreign languages.* NY: Modern Language Association.

Allport, G.W. (1954). *The nature of prejudice.* Reading, MA: Addison-Wesley.

American Council of Teachers of Foreign Languages: Performance guidelines: Draft. (1998). Yonkers, NY: ACTFL.

American Council of Teachers of Foreign Languages: K-12 Performance Guidelines. (1998). *Foreign Language Annals, 31* (4), 484.

American Council of Teachers of Foreign Languages: K-12 Performance guidelines. (1999). Yonkers, NY: ACTFL.

Andrade, C., Kretschmer, R., & Kretschmer, L. (1989). Two languages for all children: Expanding to low achievers and the handicapped. In K. E. Muller (Ed.). *Languages in elementary schools,* (pp. 177-203). New York: The American Forum.

Armstrong, E. (1998). Summer Language Immersion Day Camps. In *A Celebration of FLES*,* G. Lipton (Ed.). Lincolnwood, IL: NTC Publishing Company.

Armstrong. P., & Rogers, J. (1997). Basic skills revisited: The effects of foreign language instruction on reading, math, and language arts. *Learning Languages,* 2 (3): 20-31.

Asher, J., & Garcia, R. (1969). The optimal age to learn a foreign language. *Modern Language Journal, 53,* 334-341.

Asher, J., & Price, B. (1967). The learning strategy of total physical response: Some age differences. *Child Development, 38,* 1219-1227.

Baker, C. (1995). *A parents' and teachers' guide to bilingualism.* United Kingdom: Multilingual Matters.

Bamford, K., & Mizokawa, D. (1991). Additive-bilingual (immersion) education: cognitive and language development. *Language Learning 41* (3), 413-429.

Banks, J. (1994). *An introduction to multicultural education.* Needham Heights, MA: Allyn and Bacon.

Banks, J.A. (1991b). *Teaching strategies for ethnic studies* (5th ed.). Boston, MA: Allyn & Bacon.

Banks, J.A., & Lynch, J. (Eds.). (1986). *Multicultural education in western societies.* London: Holt, Rinehart, & Winston.

Baranick, W., & Markham, P. (1986). Attitudes of elementary school principals towards foreign language instruction. *Foreign Language Annals, 19* (4), 481-489.

Barnett, H. (1986). Foreign language for younger students and foreign language for ALL students: A perfect marriage. *Language Association Bulletin, New York State Association of Foreign Language Teachers, 37 (3),* 5.

Barnett, H., & Reardon, P. (1999). FLES programs in New York State. *Language Association Bulletin, 50* (4), NY: New York State Association of Foreign Language Teachers.

Begley, S. (1996, February 19). Your child's brain. *Newsweek,* pp. 55-62.

Bennett, S.N. (1975). Weighing the evidence: A review of "Primary French in the balance." *British Journal of Educational Psychology, 45,* 337-40.

Bergentoft, R. (1994). Foreign language instruction: A comparative perspective. *The Annals of The American Academy of Political and Social Science, 532*, 9-34.

Bishop, J. (1993, October 12). Word processing: Research on stoke victims yields clues to the brain's capacity to create language. *The Wall Street Journal,* pp. A1, A14.

Blakeslee, S. (1991, September 10). Brain yields clues to its organization for language. *The New York Times,* pp. C1, C10-11.

Blakeslee, S. (1995, September 26). Traffic jams in brain networks may result in verbal stumbles. *The New York Times,* pp. C1. C9-14.

Blakeslee, S. (1997, July 15). When an adult adds a language, it's one brain, two systems. *The New York Times,* p. C4.

Boston, C. (1998). Federal support for foreign language education. *ERIC Review, 6* (1), 42-43.

Branaman, L., & Rhodes, N. (1997). *A national survey of foreign language instruction in elementary schools.* Washington, DC: Center for Applied Linguistics.

Brecht, R., & Walton, A. R. (1995). The future shape of language learning in the new world of global communication: Consequences for higher education and beyond. In R.

Donato & R. Terry (Eds.), *Foreign language learning: The journey of a lifetime.* Lincolnwood, IL: National Textbook Company.

Brega, E., & Newell, J. (1967). High school performance of FLES and non-FLES students. *Modern Language Journal, 51,* 408-411.

Browder, L. (1995). An alternative to the doctoral dissertation: The policy advocacy concept and the doctoral policy document. *Journal of School Leadership, 5*, 40-68.

Brown, C. (1994). Elementary school foreign language programs in the United States. *The Annals of The American Academy of Political and Social Science, 532*, 164-176.

Bruck, M., Lambert, E., & Tucker, G. (1974). Bilingual schooling through the elementary grades: The St. Lambert project at grade seven. *Learning Language, 24* (2), 183-204.

Burrill, C. (1985). *The sensitive period hypothesis: A review of literature regarding acquisition of a native-like pronunciation in a second language.* (Report No. FL 015 473). Bellevue, WA: Paper presented at meeting of TRI-TESOL Conference. (ERIC Document Reproduction Service No. ED 265 7450)

Burstall, C., Jamieson, M., Cohen, S., & Hargreaves, M. (1974). *Primary French in the balance.* Windsor: National Foundation for Educational Research.

Caldas, S., & Boudreaux, N. (1999). Poverty, race, and foreign language immersion: Predictors of math and English language arts performance. *Learning Languages 5* (1), p. 4-15.

Campbell, R., Gray, T., Rhodes, N., & Snow, M. (1985). Foreign language learning in the elementary schools: A comparison of three language programs.

Modern Language Journal, 69, 44-51.

Campbell, W. (1962). *Some effects of teaching foreign language in the elementary schools.* Hicksville, New York: New York State Department of Education. (ERIC Document Reproduction Service No. ED 013 022)

Carpenter, J., & Torney, J. (1974). Beyond the melting pot. In P. M. Markun. *Childhood and intercultural education: Overview and research.* Washington, DC: Association for Childhood Education International.

Cloud, N. (1998). Teacher competencies in content-based instruction. In M. Met, (Ed.), *Critical issues in early language learning* (113-123). New York: Scott Foresman-Addison Wesley.

Cohen, J. (1965). Some statistical issues in psychological research. In B. B. Wolman (Ed.), *Handbook of clinical psychology.* New York: McGraw-Hill.

College Entrance Examination Board. (1992). *College-bound seniors. 1992 profile of SAT and achievement test takers. National report.* New York: College Entrance Examination Board. (ERIC Document Reproduction Service No. ED 351 352)

Collier, V. (1989). How long? A synthesis of research on academic achievement in a second language. *TESOL Quarterly, 23,* 509-531.

Cooper, H. *Synthesizing research: A guide for literature reviews (3rd Ed.).* Thousand Oaks, CA: Sage Publications.

Cooper, T. (1987). Foreign language study and SAT-verbal scores. *Modern Language Journal, 71* (4), 2-8.

Corbin, S., & Chiachiere, F. (1997). Attitudes toward and achievement in foreign language study. *Educational Research Quarterly, 21* (1), 3-13.

Crandall, J., & Tucker, R. (1990). Content- based instruction in second and foreign languages. In A. Padilla, H. Fairchild, & C. Valdez (Eds.) *Foreign language education issues & strategies* (pp. 187-200). Newbury Park, CA: Sage Publications.

Cummins, J. (1981). The role of primary language development in promoting educational success of language minority students. In *Schooling and language minority students: A theoretical framework* (p. 3-49). Los Angeles, CA: Evaluation, Dissemination, and Assessment Center, California State University.

Cummins, J. (1983b). *Heritage language education: A literature review.* Toronto: Ontario Ministry of Education.

Cummins, J. (1984). *Bilingualism and special education: Issues in assessment and pedagogy.* Clevedon, England: Multilingual Matters.

Curtain, H. (1998). When should an elementary foreign language program begin? In M. Met (Ed.), *Critical issues in early second language learning* (pp. 24-26). New York: Scott Foresman-Addison Wesley.

Curtain, H. (1993). *An early start: A resource book for elementary school foreign language.* Washington, DC: ERIC Clearinghouse on Languages and Linguistics. (ERIC Document Reproduction Service No. ED 353 849)

Curtain, H., & Haas, M. (1995). *Integrating foreign language and content instruction in grades K-8.* (Report No. EDO-FL-95-07). Washington, DC: ERIC Clearinghouse on Languages and Linguistics. (ERIC Document Reproduction Service No. ED 381 018)

Curtain, H., & Pesola, C. (1994). *Languages and children: Making the match.* White Plains, NY: Longman Publishing Group.

Danesi, M. (1994). The neuroscientific perspective in second language acquisition research: a critical synopsis. *IRAL, 32* (3), 201-228.

Dateline NBC, November 28, 1997, Catalogue No. NDL971128, 1 (800) 420-2626.

Di Pietro, R. (1979). Filling the elementary curriculum with languages: What are the effects? *Modern Language Journal, 63,* 192-201.

District of Columbia Public Schools. (1971). *A study of the effect of Latin instruction on English skills of the sixth grade students in the Public Schools of the District of Columbia, school year, 1970-71.* Washington, DC: Division of Planning, Research, and Evaluation. (ERIC Document Reproduction Service No. ED 060 695)

Donato, R. (1998). Assessing foreign language abilities of the early language learner. In M. Met (Ed.), *Critical issues in early second language learning* (pp. 169-175i). Glenview, IL: Scott Foresman-Addison Wesley.

Donato, R., & Terry, R. (1995). Foreign language learning: The journey of a lifetime. Lincolnwood, IL: National Textbook Company.

Donato, R., Tucker, R., & Antonek, J. (1994). A multiple perspectives analysis of a Japanese FLES program. *Foreign Language Annals, 27* (3), 365-378.

Donato, R., Tucker, R., & Antonek, J. (1996). *Monitoring and assessing a Japanese FLES program: Ambiance and achievement.* (Report No. FL 023 705). Washington D.C.: U.S. Department of Education. (ERIC Document Reproduction Service No. ED 397 632)

Donaghue, M. (1965). What research tells us about the effects of FLES. *Hispania, 48,* 555-558.

Donoghue, M. (1969). Foreign languages in the elementary school: Effects and instructional arrangements according to research. In A. W. JeKenta (Ed.), *Reports on the teaching of foreign languages*. New York: Modern Language Association.

Donoghue, M. (1981). Recent Research in FLES. *Hispania, 64,* 602-604.

Doyé, P., & Hurrell, A. (Eds.), (1997). *Foreign language learning in primary schools (pp. 7-15).* Strasbourg, France: Council of Europe Publishing.

Dulay, H., Burt, M., & Krashen, S. (1982). *Language two.* New York: Oxford University Press.

Dunkel, H., & Pillet, R. (1957). A second year of French in elementary school. *Elementary School Journal, 58,* 143-151.

Early elementary resource guide to integrated learning, University of the State of New York: New York State Education Department: 1998.

Eddy, P. (1978). *The effect of foreign language study on verbal ability in the native language: A review of evidence.* (ERIC Reproduction Service No. ED 165 469).

Eddy, P. (1981). *The effect of foreign language study in high school on verbal ability as measured by the Scholastic Aptitude Test-Verbal. Final Report.* Washington, DC: Center for Applied Linguistics. (ERIC Reproduction Services No ED 196 312).

Educate America 2000: National goals panel. (1995). *The national goals report: Executive summary.* Washington, DC: Government Printing Office.

Educating America's Children for Tomorrow Act of 1998, 106th Congress, Title IV, S. 667, Sections 401, 402. (1998).

Educational Excellence for All Children Act of 1999, 106th Congress, Title X, S. 1180, Part I, Section 10902. (1999).

ERIC Review: K-12 foreign language education. (1998). Washington, DC: ERIC Clearinghouse on Languages and Linguistics, 6(1).

Evans M., & Moritsugu, K. (1999, January 3). Welcome to Long Island. *Long Island Newsday, pp.* H16-H29.

Fathman, A. (1975). The relationship between age and second language productive ability. *Language Learning, 25* (2), 245-53.

Foreign Language Assistance for National Security Act. (1983). Committee on Education and Labor House of Representatives: Ninety-eighth congress. Washington, DC: Government Printing Office.

Fortune, T., & Jorstad, H. (1996). U.S. immersion programs: A national survey. *Foreign Language Annals, 29* (2), 163-190.

Foster, K., & Reeves, C. (1989). FLES improves cognitive skills. *FLES News, 2* (3), 4-5.

Ganschow. L., Sparks, R., Javorsky, J., Pohlman, J., & Bishop-Marury, A. (1991). Identifying native language difficulties among foreign language learners in college: A "foreign" language learning disability? *Journal of Learning Disabilities, 24* (9), 530-541.

Gardner, R., & Lambert, W. (1972). *Attitudes and motivation in second-language learning.* Rowley, MA: Newbury House.

Gardner, R., & Smythe, P. C. (1981). On the development of the Attitude/Motivation Test Battery. *Canadian Modern Language Review, 37,* 510-525.

Garfinkel, A., & Tabor, K. (1991). Elementary school foreign languages and English reading achievement: A new view of the relationship. *Foreign Language Annals, 24* (5), 375-382.

Genesee, F. (1976a). The role of intelligence in second language learning. *Language Learning, 26,* 267-280.

Genesee, F. (1976b). The suitability of French immersion programs for all children. *Canadian Modern Language Review, 32,* 494-515.

Genesee, F. (1983). Bilingual education of majority-language children: The immersion experiments in review. *Applied Psycholinguistics, 4* (1), 1-46.

Genesee, F. (1985). Second language learning through immersion: A review of U.S. programs. *Review of Educational Research, 55* (4), 541-561.

Genesee, F. (1991). Second language learning in school settings: Lessons from immersion. In A. G. Reynolds (Ed*.) Bilingualism, multiculturalism, and second language learning* (pp. 183-202). Hillsdale, NJ: Lawrence Erlbaum.

Genesee, F., Holobow, N., Wallace, E., & Chartrand, L. (1989). Three elementary school alternatives for learning through a second language. *Modern Language Journal, 73,* 250-263.

Gollnick, D.M. (1980). Multicultural education. *Viewpoints in teaching and learning, 56,* 1-17.

Gray, T., Campbell, R., Rhodes, N., Snow, M. (1984). *Comparative evaluation of the elementary foreign language programs. Final report.* (Report No. FL 225 403). Washington D.C.: Center for Applied Linguistics. (ERIC Document Reproduction Service No. ED 238 255)

Haas, M. (1999). *Thematic, communicative language teaching and learning: Case studies of FLES teachers and their classes.* Doctoral Dissertation: Teachers' College, Columbia University.

Hakuta, K. (1986). *Mirror of language: The debate on bilingualism.* New York: Basic Books.

Hancock, C., Lipton, G., & Baslow, A. (1976). A study of FLES and non-FLES pupils' attitudes toward the French and their culture. *French Review, 49* (5), 717-22.

Harley, B. (1986). *Age in second language acquisition.* San Diego, CA: College-Hill Press.

Harley, B. (1998). The outcomes of early and later language learning. In M. Met (Ed), *Critical issues in early second language learning* (pp. 26-31). Glenview, IL: Scott Foresman-Addison Wesley.

Harley, B., & Hart, D. (1997). Language aptitude and second language proficiency in classrooms learners of different starting ages. *Studies in second language acquisition, 19,* 379-400.

Heining-Boynton, A. (1990). The development and testing of the FLES program evaluation inventory. *Modern Language Journal, 74,* 432-439.

Heining-Boynton, A. (1991). FLES program evaluation: Rationale and procedural design. In: *Acting on priorities: A commitment to excellence. Report of Southern Conference on Language Teaching.* (Report No. FL 020 470) Washington, DC: Office of Educational Research and Improvement. (ERIC Document Reproduction Service No. ED 348 854)

Heining-Boynton, A. (1994). The at-risk student in the foreign language classroom. In G. Crouse, (Ed.), *Meeting new challenges in the foreign language classroom* (pp. 21-38), Lincolnwood, IL: National Textbook Company.

Heining-Boynton, A. (1998). What are the advantages and disadvantages of FLES, FLEX, and Immersion. In M. Met (Ed.), *Critical issues in early second language learning* (pp. 1-23). Glenview, IL: Scott Foresman-Addison Wesley.

Herricks Union Free School District. (1998). *Mission Statement*. New Hyde

Heining-Boynton, D. (1991). The developing child: What every FLES teacher needs to know. In L. Strasheim (Ed.), *Central states conference on the teaching of foreign languages: Focus on the foreign language learner: Priorities and strategies* (pp. 3-11). Lincolnwood, IL: National Textbook Company.

Park, NY: Herricks Union Free School District.

Hoch, F. (1998). A view from the state level. In M. Met (Ed.), *Critical issues in early second language learning* (pp. 5-10). Glenview, IL: Scott Foresman-Addison Wesley.

Holobow, N., Genesee, F., & Lambert, W. (1987). Effectiveness of partial French immersion for children from different social class and ethnic backgrounds. *Applied Linguistics, 8,* 137-52.

Holobow, N., Genesee, F., & Lambert, W. (1991). The effectiveness of a foreign language program for children from different ethnic and social class backgrounds: Report 2. *Applied Psycholinguistics, 12,* 179-198.

Interview with an LD/FL Instructor: How a teacher uses her own LD recipe for success. (1999, Spring). *ACTFL Newsletter, 11,* (3), 1,6.

Johnston, C., & Dainton, G. (1996). *Learning Combination Inventory*. Pittsgrove, NJ: Let Me Learn, Inc.

Johnson, C., Flores, J., & Ellison, F. (1961). The effect of foreign language instruction on basic learning in elementary schools. *Modern Language Journal, 45 (5),* 200-202.

Johnson, C., Flores, J., & Ellison, F. (1963). The effect of foreign language instruction on basic learning in elementary schools. *Modern Language Journal, 47 (1),* 8-11.

Johnson, J., & Newport, E. (1989). Critical period effects in second language learning: The influence of maturational state on the acquisition of English as a second language. *Cognitive Psychology, 21,* 60-99.

Krashen, S. (1981). *Second language acquisition and second language learning.* New York: Pergamon Press.

Krashen, S., Long, M., & Scarcella, C. (1979). Age, rate and eventual attainment in second language acquisition. *TESOL Quarterly, 13* (4), 573-582.

Krashen, S., Long, M., & Scarcella, C. (1982). *Child-adult differences in second language acquisition.* Rowley, MA: Newbury House Publishers.

Lambert, W., & Klineberg, O. (1967). *Children's views of foreign peoples: A cross-national study.* New York: Appleton-Century-Crofts.

Landry, R., (1973a). The enhancement of figural creativity through second language learning in the elementary school level. *Foreign Language Annals, 7,* 111-115.

Landry, R. (1973b). The relationship of second language learning and verbal creativity. *Modern Language Journal, 57,* 110-113.

Landry, R. (1974). A comparison of second language learners and monolinguals in divergent thinking tasks at the elementary school level. *Modern*

Language Journal, 58, 10-15.

   Lawrence Public Schools, Foreign Language in the Elementary School, Report and Recommendations. (1999). Lawrence, NY: Lawrence Public Schools, 195 Broadway, Lawrence, NY 11559.

   Leino, W.B., & Haak, L. (1993). *The teaching of Spanish in the elementary schools and the effects on achievement in other selected areas.* (U.S. Department of Health, Education, and Welfare, Office of Education, Contract SAE 9515). St. Paul, MN: St. Paul Public Schools.

   LeLoup, J., & Ponterio, R. (1998). Using the Internet for foreign language instruction. *ERIC Review, 6* (1), 60-61.

   Lenneberg, E. (1967). *Biological foundations of language.* New York: Wiley.

   Lipton, G. (1998). *Practical handbook to elementary foreign language programs* (4th ed.). Lincolnwood, IL: National Textbook Company.

   Lipton, G., Morgan, R., & Reed, M. (1996). Does FLES* help AP French students perform better? *AATF National Bulletin, 21,* 4.

   Lipton, G. (1994). FLES programs today: Options and opportunities. *The French Review, 68* (1), 1-16.

   Lipton, G. (1996). The politics of change: Implementation of FLEX in the public schools of Gilbert, AZ: Hispania, *29* (2), 621-626.

   Lipton, G. (1998). A century of progress. A retrospective on FLES programs: 1898-1998. *Hispania, 81,* 75-87.

   United States Census Reports for Nassau and Suffolk Counties. (1999). Long Island Regional Planning Board. 100 Veterans Highway, Hauppauge, New York.

Long, M. (1990). Maturational constraints on language development. *SSLA, 12,* 251-285.

Lopato, E. (1963). FLES and academic achievement. *French Review, 36,* 499-507.

Lorenz, E., & Met, M. (1990). *Teaching mathematics and science in the immersion classroom. Teacher's activity manual.* (Report No. FL 021 173). Washington, D.C.: Department of Education. (ERIC Document Reproduction Service No. ED 356 664)

Margarita, E. (1998). FLES programs on Long Island. *LILT Newsletter.* NY: Long Island Language Teachers.

Margarita, E. (1999). FLES programs on Long Island. *LILT Newsletter.* NY: Long Island Language Teachers.

Masciantonio, R. (1977). Tangible benefits of the study of Latin: A review of the research. *Foreign Language Annals, 10,* 375-382.

Mavrogenes, N. A. (1979). Latin in the elementary school: A help for reading and language arts. *Phi Delta Kappan, 60,* 675-77.

Mayeux, A., & Dunlap, J. (1966). *French language achievement: The effect of early language instruction on subsequent achievement.* University City, MO: University City School District. (ERIC Document Reproduction Service No. ED 070 759)

McCaig, R. (1988). *The effect of the elementary foreign language program on aspects of elementary education: a longitudinal study.* Ferndale, MI: Ferndale Public Schools.

McClendon, L., & Uchilara, A. (1998). Articulation: lessons from the past, planning for the future. In M. Met (Ed.), *Critical issues in early second language learning* (pp. 152-157). Glenview, IL: Scott Foresman-Addison Wesley.

Met, M. (1989). Which foreign languages should students learn? *Educational Leadership, 46* (6), 54-58.

Met, M. (1990). Elementary school foreign language instruction: Priorities for the 1990's. *Foreign Language Annals, 23* (5), 433-443.

Met, M. (1994). Foreign language policy in U.S. secondary schools: Who decides? *The Annals of The American Academy of Political and Social Science, 532,* 149-163.

Met, M. (1998). *Critical issues in early language learning.* New York: Scott Foresman-Addison Wesley.

Met, M., & Rhodes, N. (1990). Priority: Instruction. Elementary school foreign language instruction: Priorities for the 1990s. *Foreign Language Annals,* 23 (5): 433-43.

Mills, Richard. (July, 10, 1998). *Letter to the members of the board of Regents of New York State.* Albany, NY: The State Education Department of the University of the State of New York.

Muller, K. (1989). (Ed.). *Languages in elementary schools.* New York, NY: The American Forum.

Munks, J. (1996). The case for multilingual citizens in the 21st century. In B. Wing (Ed.), *Foreign languages for all: Challenges and choices* (pp. 1-18). Lincolnwood, IL: National Textbook Company.

Myers, I. B., & McCaulley, M. H. (1985). *Manual: A guide to the development and use of the Myers-Briggs Type Indicator.* Palo Alto, CA: Consulting Psychologists Press.

Nash, J. (1997, February 3). Fertile minds. *Time, 149* (5), 49-56.

Nespor, H. (1970). The effect of foreign language learning on expressive productivity in native oral language. (Doctoral Dissertation, University of

California, Berkeley, 1969). *Dissertation Abstracts International, 31* (02-A), 128.

New York State Association of Foreign Languages Teachers. (April, 1998). *International Comparisons*. New York: NYSAFLT.

New York State Department of Education. (1996). *Learning standards for languages other than English*. Albany, NY: The University of the State of New York.

New York State Foreign Language Implementation Committee. (1998). *Report of the Foreign Language Implementation Committee*. Albany, NY: New York State Education Department.

New York State Graduation Requirements. (1998). *A summary of Regents report on graduation requirements*. Albany, NY: State Education Department.

Newport, E. (1990). Maturation constraints on language learning. *Cognitive Science, 14*, 11-28.

Offenberg, R. (1971*). Evaluation of the elementary school (FLES) Latin program 1970-1971*. Office of Research and Evaluation. Philadelphia, PA: The School District of Philadelphia. (ERIC Document Reproduction Service No. ED 056 612)

Olson, L., & Samuels, S. J. (1973). The relationship between age and accuracy of foreign language pronunciation. *The Journal of Educational Research, 66* (6), 263-268.

Omaggio-Hadley, A. (1993). *Teaching language in context*. Boston, MA: Heinle and Heinle.

Orringer, C. (1998). Reaching a decision on the appropriate model. In M. Met (Ed.), *Critical issues in early second language learning* (pp. 12-15). Glenview, IL: Scott Foresman-Addison Wesley.

Osterman, K., & Kottkamp, R. (1993). *Reflective practice for educators: Improving schooling through professional development.* Newbury Park, CA: Corwin Press.

Owston, R.D. (1997). The World Wide Web: A technology to enhance teaching and learning? *Educational Researcher, 3,* 27-33.

Oyama, S. (1976). A sensitive period for the acquisition of a nonnative phonological system. *Journal of Psycholinguistic Research, 5* (3), 261-285.

Oxford, R. (1998). Uses of advanced technology for early language learning. In M. Met (Ed.), *Critical issues in early second language learning* (pp. 137-144). Glenview, IL: Scott Foresman-Addison Wesley.

Peal, E., & Lambert, W. (1962). Bilingualism and intelligence. *Psychological Monographs, 76* (27), 546.

Peck, K., & Dorricott, D. (1994). Why use technology? *Educational Leadership, 51* (7). 11-14.

Penfield, W. (1964). The uncommitted cortex: A child's changing brain. *Atlantic Monthly, 214,* 77-81.

Penfield, W., & Roberts, L. (1959). *Speech and brain mechanisms.* Princeton, NJ: Princeton University Press.

Pesola, C. (1995). Background, design and evaluation of a conceptual framework for FLES curriculum. (Doctoral Dissertation, University of Minnesota, 1995). *Dissertation Abstracts International, A 56* (12*),* 4653.

Philips, J. (1994). State and local policy on the study of foreign languages. *The Annals of The American Academy of Political and Social Science, 532,* 88-98.

Potts, M. (1967). The effect of second-language instruction on the reading achievement of primary grade children. *American Education Research Journal, 4,* 367-373.

Rafferty, E. (1986). *Second language study and basic skills in Louisiana.* Baton Rouge, LA: Louisiana State Department of Education. (ERIC Document Reproduction Service No. ED 283 360)

Ramirez, A. (1998). Language proficiency, cross-cultural competence, and long-term program evaluation. In M. Met (Ed.), *Critical issues in early second language learning* (pp. 324-338). NY: Scott Foresman-Addison Wesley.

Rhodes, N., & Oxford, R. (1988). *A national profile of foreign language instruction at the elementary and secondary school levels.* (Technical Report Series No. 6). Los Angeles, CA: Center for Language Education and Research. (ERIC Document Reproduction Service No. ED 291 249)

Rhodes, N., Thompson, L., & Snow, M. (1989). *A comparison of FLES and immersion programs. Final report.* (Report No. FL 017 970). Washington, DC: Center for Applied Linguistics. (ERIC Document Reproduction Services No. ED 317 031)

Riddick, L.A. (1991). A comparison of students performance in partial immersion and FLES programs. (Doctoral Dissertation, Virginia Polytech Institute, 1991). *Dissertation Abstracts International, 52* (04) A 1201.

Riestra, M., & Johnson, C. (1964). Changes in attitudes of elementary school pupils towards foreign-speaking peoples resulting from the study of a foreign language. *The Journal of Experimental Education, 33* (1), 65-72.

Riley, R. (1993). World-class standards: The key to educational reform. *Teaching K-8, 24* (2), 6.

Riley, R. (February 11, 1999). *Statement by United States Secretary of Education Richard W. Riley regarding the Educating America's Children for Tomorrow Act of 1998.* [On line], www.ed.gov/offices/OESE/ESEA/themes/cc-title-x-lang.html

Riley, R. (May 19, 1999). *Statement by United States Secretary of Education Richard W. Riley regarding the Educational Excellence for All Children Act of 1999.* Contact: Julie Green (202) 401-3026.

Rosenbusch, M. (1991). Elementary school foreign language: The establishment and maintenance of strong programs. *Foreign Language Annals, 24* (4), 297-313.

Rosenbusch, M. (1992). Is knowledge of cultural diversity enough? Global education in the elementary school foreign language program. *Foreign Language Annals, 25* (2), 129-36.

Rosenbusch, M. (1995). Language learners in the elementary school. In R. Donato & R. Terry (Eds.), *Foreign language learning: The journey of a lifetime.* (pp. 1-36). Lincolnwood, IL: National Textbook Company.

Rosenbusch, M. (Ed.). (1999). *Learning Languages, 5* (1).

Rosenzweig, C. (1999). *Parenting and school success: The role of parents in promoting students' school adjustment and scholastic performance.* Unpublished Manuscript, Hofstra University.

Schinke-Llano, L. (1985). *Foreign language in the elementary school: State of the art.* New York: Harcourt, Brace & Jovanovich.

Schrier, L., & Fast, M. (1992). Foreign Language in the elementary schools and computer-assisted language learning. *Hispania, 75,* 1304-1311.

Schuman, J. (1975). Affective factors and the problem of age in second language acquisition. *Language Learning, 25* (2), 209-235.

Seelye, H. (1981). *Teaching culture.* Lincolwood, IL: National Textbook Company.

Senge, P. (1990). *The fifth discipline.* New York: Doubleday.

Sheridan, R. (1976). *Augmenting skills through language learning transfer.* (Report No. FL 008 366). Indianapolis, IN: Indianapolis Public Schools. (ERIC Document Reproduction Service No. ED 135 218)

Shohamy, E. (1997). *Critical language testing.* Plenary session presented at the 1997 meeting of the American Association of Applied Linguistics, Orlando, FL.

Shrum, J. (1985). *An ethnographic evaluation of a FLES program.* (Report No. FL 015 572). Washington, D.C.: U.S. Department of Education. (ERIC Document Reproduction Service No. ED 267 620)

Singleton, D., & Lengyel, Z. (Eds.). (1995*). The age factor in second language acquisition.* Philadelphia, PA: Multilingual Matters.

Slavin R. (19950. *Cooperative Learning.* Needham Heights, MA: Simon & Schuster Company.

Snow, M. (1985). *Student questionnaire.* Los Angeles: University of California. Unpublished document.

Snow, C., & Hoefnagel-Hohle, M. (1978). The critical period for language acquisition: Evidence from second language learning. *Child Development, 49,* 1114-1128.

Snow, M., Met, M., & Genesee, F. (1989). A conceptual framework for the integration of language and content instruction. *TESOL Quarterly, 23* (2), 201-217.

Sparks, R., & Ganschow, L. (1993). The impact of native language learning problems on foreign language learning: Case study illustrations of the linguistic coding deficit hypothesis. *Modern Language Journal, 77* (1), 68-71.

Sparks, R., Ganschow, L., Kenneweg, S., & Miller, K. (1991). Use of an Orton-Gillingham approach to teach a foreign language to dyslexic/learning -disabled students: Explicit teaching of phonology in a second language. *Annals of Dyslexia, 42,* 97-114.

Spinelli, E. (1996). Meeting the challenges of the diverse secondary school population. In B. Wing (Ed.) *Foreign languages for all: Challenges and choices* (pp. 57-87). Lincolnwood, IL: National Textbook Company.

Standards for foreign language learning: Preparing for the 21st century. (1996). Lawrence, KA: Allen Press.

Stern, H. (1976). Optimal age: Myth or reality? *Canadian Modern Language Review,* 32: 283-94.

Swain, M. (1981). Linguistic expectations: Core, extended and immersion programs. *The Canadian Modern Language Review,* 37 (3): 486-97.

Swain, M. (1981). Time and timing in bilingual education. *Language Learning, 31,* 1-15.

Tedrick, D., & Walker, C. (1996). R(T)eaching all students: Necessary changes in teacher education. In B. Wing (Ed.) *Foreign languages for all: Challenges and choices* (pp. 187-220). Lincolnwood, IL: National Textbook Company.

Thompson, L. (1988). *The development of the FLES test—Spanish. Final report.* (Report No. FL 019 760). Washington, D.C.: Office of Educational Research and Improvement. (ERIC Document Reproduction Services No. ED 337 042)

Thompson, L. (1995). *K-8 foreign language assessment: A bibliography.* (Report No. FL 023 181). Washington, DC: Office of Educational Research and Improvement. (ERIC Document Reproduction Service No. ED 385 165)

Thompson, L., Christian, D., Stansfield, C., & Rhodes, N. (1990). Foreign language instruction in the United States. In A. Padilla, H. Fairchild, & C. Valdez (Eds.), *Foreign language education: Issues and strategies* (pp. 22-37). Newbury Park, CA: Sage.

Toulmin, S. (1971). Human Understanding. Princeton, NJ: University Press.

Trugly, S., & Garcia, P. (1998). On planning, staff development, and multicultural issues: A principal's perspective. In M. Met (Ed.), *Critical issues in early second language learning* (pp. 216-221). Glenview, IL: Scott Foresman-Addison Wesley.

Tucker, R. (1990). Second language education: Issues and perspective. In A. Padilla, H. Fairchild, & C. Valdez (Eds.) *Foreign language education: Issues and strategies* (pp.13-21). Newbury Park, NJ: Sage.

Tucker, G., Donato, R., & Antonek, J. (1995). *Documenting an exemplary Japanese FLES program: In pursuit of goals 2000.* (Report No. FL 023 271). Pittsburgh, PA: Carnegie Mellon University. (ERIC Document Reproduction Service No. ED 386 954)

Two-Way Immersion Directory. (1999). Center for Applied Linguistics, 4646 40th Street, Washington, DC. [On line] www.twi.cal.org

U.S. Department of Education. (1996). *Standards for foreign language learning: Preparing for the 21st century.* Lawrence, KA: Allen Press Inc.

Vocolo, J. (1967). The effect of foreign language study in the elementary school upon achievement in the same foreign language in the high school. *Modern Language Journal, 51*, 463-70.

Vollmer, J. H. (1962). *Evaluation of the effects of FLES upon achievement in the high school: Final report. Somerville, NJ: Board of Education.*

Vygotsky, L. (1986). *Thought and language.* Cambridge, MA: MIT Press.

Watzke, J., & Grundstad, D. (1996). Student reasons for studying foreign language: Implications for program planning and development. *Learning Languages, 2* (1), 15-29.

Weatherford, H.J. (1986). Personal benefits of foreign language study. *ERIC Digest.* Washington, DC: ERIC Clearinghouse on Languages and Linguisitics, (ERIC Document Reproduction Service No. 276 305)

Wehlage, G.G., & Rutter, R.A. (1986). Dropping out: how much do schools contribute to the problem? *Teachers College Record, 87* (3), 374-392.

Winslow, O. (1999, November 7). Making every word count. *Long Island Newsday,* pp. A19, A61.

Winslow, R. (1997, July 10). How language is stored in the brain depends on age. *The Wall Street Journal, B1*, B6.

Wilburn, D. (1990). *Syllabus for a FLES methods course.* Washington, DC: U.S. Department of Education. (ERIC Document Reproduction Service No. ED 336 946)

Wing, B. (Ed.) *Foreign languages for all: Challenges and choices.* Lincolnwood, IL: National Textbook Company.

Yamada, J., Takatsuka, S., Kotake, N., & Kurusu, J. (1980). On the optimum age for teaching foreign vocabulary to children. *IRAL, 18* (3), 245-247.

Yerkes, D. (Ed.). (1989). *The Webster's encyclopedic unabridged dictionary of the English language.* New York: Crown Publishers.

Yerxa, E. (1970). Attitude development in childhood education toward foreign people. *Journal of Education, 152,* 23-33.

Zlokower, R. (1991) *Toward nurturing foreign languages in elementary schools in New York State: Programs and options.* Dissertation, New York: Columbia Teachers College.

Appendix A

K-6 Sequential FLES Programs in Public Schools on Long Island (as of 2003)

District	Year Started	Grades	Schedule	Language	# Schools	# Teachers	Full/ Part time
Amagansett*	1987	PreK-6	Pre K=2 x 30 min. K-6=2 x 40 min.	Spanish	1	1	ft
Babylon	1998	K-6	K-1=2 x 20 min. 2-6=alt. day 20 min.	K-3 Spn 4-6 Fr/Spn	2	1/2	ft/pt
Bellmore	2000	1-5	1-5=2 x 30	Spanish	4	3	ft
East Islip*	1998	K-6	K-5=3 x 25 min. or 2 x 35/40 min. 6=2 x 35/40 min.	Spanish	5	8	ft
Fishers Island	1996	K-6	2 x 20 min.	Spanish	1	1	ft
Lawrence*	1999	K-2	K=2 x 30 min. 1-2=3 x 30 min.	Spanish	5	4	ft
Manhasset	2000	K-3	3 x 20 min.	Spanish	2	3	ft
Mineola*	1997	3-5	3 x 35 min.	Spanish	1 of 4	1	ft
Montauk	2001	K-5	2 x 40 min.	Spanish	1	2	ft
Oceanside*	1997	K-6	K-5=alt. day 20 min. 6=2 x 40 min.	Spanish	6	5	ft
Plainview*	1996	1-3	1 x 40 min.	Chinese	4	3	ft
Quogue*	1988	PreK-6	PreK=2 x 20 min. K-3=2 x 25 min. 4-6=2 x 25, 1x 45 min.	Spanish	1	1	pt
Remsenburg*	1996	K-6	K-3=2 x 30 min. 4-6=3 x 30 min.	Spanish	1	1	ft
Roslyn*	1994	K-5	K=2 x 20 min. 1-5=1 x 30 min.	Spanish	3	3	ft
Southampton*	1995	K-4	K-1=5 x 20 min. 2=2 x 30 min. 3-4=2 x 40 min.	Spanish	1	3	ft
Valley Stream No. 24*	1965	2-6	2=1 x 30 min. 3=2 x 30 min. 4-6=3 x 30 min.	Spanish	3 of 9	2	ft
Wainscott	1998	1-3	2 x 40 min.	Spanish	1	1	ft
West Babylon**	1988	3-6	3-5=1 x 40 min. 6=3 x 45 min.	Russian	5	2	ft
West Hampton*	1994	K-5	K-2=2 x 20 min. 3-5=2 x 30 min.	Spanish	1	1	ft

*Districts included in interviews conducted for this study.

Most of these districts plan to spiral up and/or down into the other grade levels.

**This district offers the FLES program to "gifted" students.

Appendix B

Foreign Language Programs Starting Before Grade 7 in Public Schools on Long Island, New York

DISTRICT	PHONE NO.	WORLD LANGUAGE SUPERVISOR	WORLD LANGUAGE PROGRAM	NUMBER OF SCHOOLS	LANGUAGE(S) OFFERED	TIMES PER WEEK	MINUTES PER SESSION	NUMBER OF TEACHERS	YEAR BEGAN (approx.)
Amagansett (Shirley)	(631) 267-3572		Pre K-6	1	Spanish	2 x a week	Pre K=30 min. K-6=40 minutes	1 Full Time	1987
Babylon	(631) 893-7900	Elaine Katsikas	K-1 & 2-6 FLES	2	K-3 Spanish 4-6 Fr or Spn	K-1=2 x 2-6=alt. day	20 minutes	1 Full Time 2 Part Time	1998
Baldwin	(516) 377-9321	Melisa Maurici	6th Grade	1	Fr, It, Latin, Spn	Alt. day/10 weeks each	40 minutes	2 Full Time	2001
Bay Shore (Dual Language)	(631) 968-1269	Ms. Haller	K-2 3-5/ 1 class in each grade level	2	Spanish	Everyday	½ time interrelated with English	2 Full Time in each school	1991
Bellmore	(516) 679-2914	Leslie Edelman	1-5 6th Grade	K-1 Childhood Center & 3 schools	Spanish Fr/Spn (10 weeks each)	2 x a week	30 minutes 40 minutes	3 Full Time	2000
Bethpage	(516) 733-3770	Alan Levine	6th Grade FLEX Plan to Spiral Down to Grade 5 – 2003	Middle School	ASL, French, Italian, Latin, Spanish	2-3 x a week 10 weeks each	45 minutes	11 Full Time	1995
Bridgehampton	(631) 537-0271 x223	Ms. Lennon	Pre K-6	1	French, Spanish (½ year of each)	1 x a week	½ hour	2 Full Time	1988
Carle Place	(516) 622-6408	Miriam Hirsch	After school, Grades 1-2	1	French, Spanish	1 x a week	1 hour	4	2000
Cold Spring Harbor	(631) 692-8600	Kathy Porter	After School, Grades 4-6	2	French, Spanish	2 x a week	35-40 minutes	Certified teachers. Not necessarily from district.	1998
Commack	(631) 912-3547	John Maher	K-5 5 week program (Feb-April) After school	3	ASL, French, German, Italian, Spanish	2 x a week	75 minutes	Depends on enrollment. Teachers from all over.	1998
Comsewogue	(631) 474-8200	Dr. Susan Fishbein	5th & 6th Grade	4 elementary 6th grade in middle school	5th=Chinese, Fr, Italian, Spanish French, Italian, Spanish	Every other day Every other day	40 minutes 43 minutes	(4) 5th grade Full Time PT Chinese 4 (shared)	1999

Appendix B

Foreign Language Programs Starting Before Grade 7 in Public Schools on Long Island, New York

DISTRICT	PHONE NO.	WORLD LANGUAGE SUPERVISOR	WORLD LANGUAGE PROGRAM	NUMBER OF SCHOOLS	LANGUAGE(S) OFFERED	TIMES PER WEEK	MINUTES PER SESSION	NUMBER OF TEACHERS	YEAR BEGAN (approx.)
Deer Park	(631) 242-6564	Mr. Moss	5th Grade	1 intermed. grades 3-5	French, Italian, Spanish	Several times on rotating basis	30-40 minutes	1 Full time Travels between buildings	1998
Dix Hills (Half Hollow Hills)	(631) 592-3189	Maxine Argiz	6th Grade	2 Middle Schools	French, Italian, Spanish	Every other day	43 minutes	1.4 in one school 2 in another	1999
East Hampton	(631) 329-4176	Dr. Sylvia Sulowski	5th & 6th Grade	Middle School at 5th Grade	French, Spanish	¼ of school year every day	41 minutes	2 Full Time 1 Part Time	1996
East Islip	(631) 581-1600 x327	Dr. Janet Hiller	K-6	5	Spanish	2-3 x week	25-40 minutes	8 Full Time	1998
East Meadow	(516) 228-5258	Gerri Doddato	6th Grade FLEX	Middle School	ASL, French, Italian, Spanish	2 x a week	39 minutes	6 Full Time Teach 6th-8th	1980's
East Rockaway	(516) 887-8310 x45	Cindy Singer	5th & 6th Grade		Italian, Spanish	5th grade= 2/10 week sessions / 6th grade	20 minutes every day / 40 minutes every other day	2 Full Time	2001
East Quogue	(631) 653-5210	Carol Talmage	5th & 6th Grade FLEX	1	French, Spanish	2 x a week	30 minutes	1 Full Time	1993
East Williston	(516) 876-4721	Jerilyn Cowen	5th Grade FLEX / 6th Grade	Intermediate School	Italian, Swahili / French, Spanish	Alt. Day / Every day	40 minutes	9 Full time 1 Part Time	1983
Eastport	(631) 325-0800	Joanne Nicodema	FLEX	1	French, Spanish (1/2 year each)	5 x a week	42 minutes	Shared with MS & HS	1996
Fishers Island	(631) 788-7444	Jim Hands	K-6	1	Spanish	K-2=2 x 3-6=2 x	20 minutes 20 minutes	1 Full Time	1996
Floral Park (Bellrose)	(516) 327-9307		4-6	2	Latin	2-3 x a week	40 minutes	Classroom teacher	1986
Freeport (Dual Language & FLEX)	(516) 867-5233	Susan Gregor	Pre K-6=Dual Language / 5th & 6th =FLEX	1	Spanish / Fr, It, Latin, Spn	5 x a week / 1 x a week	100% of day / 45 minutes	2 Full Time / 5 Part Time	1997

Margarita, 2003

Appendix B

Foreign Language Programs Starting Before Grade 7 in Public Schools on Long Island, New York

DISTRICT	PHONE NO.	WORLD LANGUAGE SUPERVISOR	WORLD LANGUAGE PROGRAM	NUMBER OF SCHOOLS	LANGUAGE(S) OFFERED	TIMES PER WEEK	MINUTES PER SESSION	NUMBER OF TEACHERS	YEAR BEGAN (approx.)
Garden City	(516) 294-3065	Mrs. Sorache	6th Grade	Middle School	French, German, Italian, Latin, Spanish	Every other day, 6 weeks of each	42 minutes	8 Full Time	1987
Great Neck South Middle School	(516) 733-1679	Toni Sanzeri	6th Grade / Optional after school	2	French, Latin, Spanish	5 x a week	42 minutes	4 Full Time 3 Part Time	1976
Hauppauge	(631) 265-3630 x389	Frank Marino	FLEX 5 / 6th Grade	3 / 1	French, German, Spanish	5 x a week, 13 weeks / 5 x a week	30 minutes / 40 minutes	2 Full Time	1984
Herricks	(516) 625-6460	Dr. Lori Ramirez	6th Grade	Middle School	French, Italian, Spanish	Semester 1/3 =5 x a week Sem. 2/4 =alt. day	42 minutes	3 Full Time (Shared)	2000
Hewlett	(516) 374-8027	Deana Schiffer	6th Grade	Middle School	French, Spanish Trimester	5 x a week	40 minutes	3 Full Time (shared)	1996
Hicksville	(516) 733-6519	Glenn Nadelback	FLEX / 6th Grade	Middle School	French, German, It, Latin Spanish	5 x a week / ½ year	40 minutes	7 (shared)	1992
Jericho	(516) 681-4100 x428	Dr. Elaine Margarita	K-5 / 6th Grade	3 / Middle School	K – rotation 1-Latin, 2-Spn, 3-Chinese, 4-Fr, 5- It / Fr, It, Spn	1 x a week / Alt. day	40 minutes / 40 minutes	3 Full Time 1 Part Time / 7	1999 / 1995
Kings Park	(631) 269-3295	Susan Rugiero	Experimental 6th Grade	1Middle School	French	5 x a week	Lunch 30 minutes	3 Full Time 1 Part Time	
Lawrence	(516) 295-8022 812-7033	Dr. Leticia Breretun	K-2	1 Pre K-K Center 4 Elementary	Spanish	K=2 x 1-2=3 x	30 minutes	4 Full Time	1999
Locust Valley	(516) 674-6367	Lori Austin	3-5	2	French, Italian, Spanish	2 x a week	40 minutes	9 shared with MS & HS	1990
Long Beach (Dual Language)	(516) 897-2067	William Van Dyke	Parents elect in Kindergarten K-5	2	Spanish	Every day including Math	½ day English ½ day Spanish	12-15 Full Time	1991

Margarita, 2003

Appendix B

Foreign Language Programs Starting Before Grade 7 in Public Schools on Long Island, New York

DISTRICT	PHONE NO.	WORLD LANGUAGE SUPERVISOR	WORLD LANGUAGE PROGRAM	NUMBER OF SCHOOLS	LANGUAGE(S) OFFERED	TIMES PER WEEK	MINUTES PER SESSION	NUMBER OF TEACHERS	YEAR BEGAN (approx.)
Lynbrook	(516) 887-0200	Lenny Bruno	6th Grade	1	Spanish		40 minutes		
Manhasset	(516) 627-8000/2441	Hedy Minerbo	K-3 (spiraling up)	2	Spanish	3 x a week	20 minutes	3 Full Time	2000
Miller Place	(631) 474-2723	Mrs. Failla	After school (SCOPE)	1	French, Italian, Spanish,	2 x a week	60 minutes	4 Full Time	2000
Mineola	(516) 741-1206	Mimi Russo	3-5	1 of 4	Spanish	3 x a week	35 minutes	1 Full Time	1996
Montauk	(631) 668-2474	J. Phillip Perna (Supt.)	K-8	1	Spanish	K-5=2 x, 6=2 x, ¾ of year 7-8=5 x	40 minutes	2 Full Time	2001
North Merrick	(516) 292-3694		After school	3	Spanish	K-1=2 x, 20 sessions 2=2 x, 16 sessions	45 minutes	1 parent	1999
North Shore	(516) 705-0232	Dr. Ellen Shields	4-5 Latin 6th Grade	Middle School	Latin / French, Italian, Latin, Spanish	3 x every 12 days / Alt. day	30 minutes / 42 minutes	2 Part Time	1993
Northport	(631) 262-6684	Larry Lubin	2-5 Grade After school	6	Spanish, French	2 x a week	40 sessions, 60 min. (Oct – May)	8 teachers	1996
Oceanside	(516) 678-7533	Dr. Elvira Morse	K-5 6th Grade	6	Spanish	Alt. day / 6th =2 x	20 minutes / 40 minutes	5 Full Time	1997
Oyster Bay	(516) 624-6552	Dr. Sal Pepitone	5th & 6th Grade	1	5= ½ yr Fr, Spn 6=Fr/Spn	Every other day	40 minutes	1 Full Time	1997
Plainview-Old Bethpage	(516) 937-6437	Elizabeth Welshofer	1-3 5= Enrichment Unit	4 2 Middle Schools	Chinese Spanish	1 x a week Every other day/10 weeks	40 minutes 42 minutes	3 Full Time .8	1996 1980s
Port Washington	(516) 767-4407	John Placella	6th Grade 5th Grade After school	1 Middle School	French, Italian, Latin, Spanish	5 x a week 1 x a week	45 minutes 60 minutes	11 MS	1996 1998

Margarita, 2003

Appendix B

Foreign Language Programs Starting Before Grade 7 in Public Schools on Long Island, New York

DISTRICT	PHONE NO.	WORLD LANGUAGE SUPERVISOR	WORLD LANGUAGE PROGRAM	NUMBER OF SCHOOLS	LANGUAGE(S) OFFERED	TIMES PER WEEK	MINUTES PER SESSION	NUMBER OF TEACHERS	YEAR BEGAN (approx.)
Port Jefferson	(631) 476-4420	Peggy Bruscia	Pre K-K 4th & 5th Grade	1	Spanish	Pre K=2 x K=1 x 4-5=alt. days	30 minutes 40 minutes 40 minutes	1 Full Time	1996
Quogue	(631) 653-4285	Richard Benson	Pre K-6	1	Spanish	Pre K=2 x K-3=2 x 4-6=3 x	20 minutes 25 minutes 2 x 40 minutes 1x 25 minutes	1 Full Time	1988
Remsenburg	(631) 325-0203	Dr. Irene Nowell	K-6	1	Spanish	K-3=2 x 4-6=3 x	30 minutes 30 minutes	1 Full Time	1996
Rockville Centre	(516) 255-8870	Risa Smith	6th Grade FLEX	Middle School	French, Spanish	6 day cycle every other day	39 minutes		
Roslyn	(516) 625-6367	Bill Ortega	K-5	3	Spanish	K=2 x a week 1-5=1x a week	K=20 minutes 1-5=30 minutes	2-3 Full Time	1994
			6th Grade	1 Middle School	Fr/Spn (½ year)	10 weeks 5 days a week	40 minutes		
Sag Harbor	(631) 725-5301	After school	K-5 3-5	1	ASL, Spanish	1 x a week 1 x a week	15 minutes 60 minutes	1	2000
Sagaponack	(631) 537-0651		2-4 After School	1	Spanish	1 x a week for 8 weeks	1 hour	1 Part Time	2000
Shelter Island	(631) 749-0302	Jeanne Cowen (Guidance Counselor)	5th Grade	K-12 Building	Spanish	Exploratory 10 weeks	40 minutes	2 Full Time	1990
South Country	(631) 286-4300	Barbara Williams	6th Grade After School	Middle School	French, Italian, Spanish	1 x a week	40 minutes	3 Full Time, during the school day	2001
South Huntington (FLEX & Dual Lang.)	(631) 425-5379 425-5387	Elizabeth Roberts	6th Grade FLEX Dual Immersion K-5	3 Languages for 13 weeks each	French, Italian, Spanish	5 x a week	42 minutes	1 Full Time 1 Part Time	1994 1991
South Manor	(631) 878-4441	Rosa Miliano	4-6	2	4-5=Spn 6=½ yr Spn ½ yr Fr	4=1 x a week 5-6=2x a week	30 minutes	4 Full Time 1 Part Time	2001

Margarita, 2003

Appendix B

Foreign Language Programs Starting Before Grade 7 in Public Schools on Long Island, New York

DISTRICT	PHONE NO.	WORLD LANGUAGE SUPERVISOR	WORLD LANGUAGE PROGRAM	NUMBER OF SCHOOLS	LANGUAGE(S) OFFERED	TIMES PER WEEK	MINUTES PER SESSION	NUMBER OF TEACHERS	YEAR BEGAN (approx.)
Southampton	(631) 283-6800 x4850	Lawrence Strickland	K-4	1	Spanish	K-1=5 x 2=3 x 3-4=2 x	K-1=20 minutes 2=30 minutes 3-4=40 minutes	3 Full Time	1995
Springs Union Free District of Easthampton	(631) 324-0144	Nancy Collins	1-5=Berlitz (workbook & tapes) 6th=6 weeks Fr/Spn	K-8 Building	French, Spanish	1-3 x a week 5 x a week	45 minutes	1 Full Time Spanish, 1 Part Time French	1998
Syosset	(516) 364-5703	Susan LoPresti	K-5 FLEX	7	Chinese, French, Italian, Spanish	2 x a week	30 minutes	9 Full Time	1997
Tuckahoe	(631) 283-3550	Carol Greenberg	FLEX Grades 3-6	1	French, Spanish (½ year each)	2 x a week	20 minutes	1 Full Time	1986
Valley Stream No. 24	(516) 285-9881	Ms. Varrone	2-6	3 of 9	Spanish	2=1 x 3=2 x 4-6=3 x in 6 day cycle	30 minutes	2 Full Time	1965
Wainscott	(631) 537-1080	Julie Matler	1-3	1	Spanish	2 x a week	40 minutes	1 Full Time	1998
Wantagh	(516) 679-6361	Pat Colasso	3-5	3	Spanish	3-4=2 x in 6 day cycle 5=3 x in 6 day cycle	40 minutes 30 minutes	2 Full Time	2000
West Babylon	(631) 321-3085 x3015	Donna Jesaitis	3-5 Grade 6th Grade	5	Russian	1 x a week 3 x a week	45 minutes 45 minutes	2 Full Time	1988
West Hempstead	(516) 390-3247	Paul Sabatino	6th Grade FLEX	1 Middle School	French, Italian, Latin, Spanish	Every other day	43 minutes	3 Shared	1997
Westbury (Dual Language)	(516) 876-5027	Dr. Toledo	1-2 (spiraling up)	2	Spanish	1	45 minutes	1	2000

Margarita, 2003

Appendix B

Foreign Language Programs Starting Before Grade 7 in Public Schools on Long Island, New York

DISTRICT	PHONE NO.	WORLD LANGUAGE SUPERVISOR	WORLD LANGUAGE PROGRAM	NUMBER OF SCHOOLS	LANGUAGE(S) OFFERED	TIMES PER WEEK	MINUTES PER SESSION	NUMBER OF TEACHERS	YEAR BEGAN (approx.)
Westhampton Beach	(631) 288-3800	Rosemary Columbia	K-5 FLES 6th Grade	1	Spanish French, Spanish	K-2=2 x 3-5=2 x 6=5 x a week	20 minutes 30 minutes ½ year exploratory	1 Full Time	1994 1991
West Islip	(631) 893-3250 x244	Elaine Korb	5th & 6th Grade FLEX	6	French, German, Italian, Spanish	½ year, 1 x a week 6th grade=10 weeks Fr, It, Spn alt. day	40 minutes	1 Part Time, 2/5 teacher	1996
William Floyd District	(631) 874-1257	Margaret Klein Helen Stopak	Dual K-2	2 (housed in one school)	Spanish	5 days a week	All day	½ day 2 teachers, team teaching	3rd year of 3 year grant

Summary of data from Appendices A and B:

Total number of schools with foreign language before grade 7	
Nassau County	34
Suffolk County	36
All Long Island Schools (N=127)	70 (55% of all Long Island Schools)

Total number of schools with various K-5 foreign language programs	
Sequential FLES	19 (9=Nassau; 9=Suffolk)
K-5 FLEX	2 (Both Nassau)
Gifted program	1 (Nassau)
All models	22 (17% of all Long Island Schools)

School Districts with Immersion Programs	6=5% of all schools (3 Nassau; 3 Suffolk)

If you would like to add, delete, or update any information in these charts, please send information to:
Dr. Elaine Margarita, via email: etmrpb@yahoo.com

Standards for
Foreign Language Learning

COMMUNICATION
Communicate in Languages
Other Than English

Standard 1.1: Students engage in conversations, provide and obtain information, express feelings and emotions, and exchange opinions.

Standard 1.2: Students understand and interpret written and spoken language on a variety of topics.

Standard 1.3: Students present information, concepts, and ideas to an audience of listeners or readers on a variety of topics.

CULTURES
Gain Knowledge and
Understanding of Other Cultures

Standard 2.1: Students demonstrate an understanding of the relationship between the practices and perspectives of the culture studied.

Standard 2.2: Students demonstrate an understanding of the relationship between the products and perspectives of the culture studied.

CONNECTIONS
Connect with Other Disciplines and
Acquire Information

Standard 3.1: Students reinforce and further their knowledge of other disciplines through the foreign language.

Standard 3.2: Students acquire information and recognize the distinctive viewpoints that are only available through the foreign language and its cultures.

COMPARISONS
Develop Insight into the Nature of
Language and Culture

Standard 4.1: Students demonstrate understanding of the nature of language through comparisons of the language studied and their own.

Standard 4.2: Students demonstrate understanding of the concept of culture through comparisons of the cultures studied and their own.

COMMUNITIES
Participate in Multilingual Communities
at Home and Around the World

Standard 5.1: Students use the language both within and beyond the school setting.

Standard 5.2: Students show evidence of becoming life-long learners by using the language for personal enjoyment and enrichment.

Standards for Foreign Language Learning **9**

Appendix D

Early Language Programs
"What the United States Can Learn from Other Countries"

INTERNATIONAL EDUCATION WEEK
STATEMENT BY U.S. SECRETARY OF STATE COLIN L. POWELL

During International Education Week, November 12-16, the Department of State recognizes the role that international education and exchange play in strengthening our nation and our relations with other countries.

Among the State Department's best-known activities is the Fulbright scholarship program, which since its inception, has given nearly a quarter of a million Americans and foreign citizens the opportunity to study and teach abroad. We are proud that the high quality of American colleges and universities attracts students and scholars from around the world. These American colleges and universities enrich our communities with their academic abilities and cultural diversity, and they return home with an increased understanding and often a lasting affection for the U.S. I can think of no more valuable asset to our country than the friendship of future world leaders who have been educated here.

At the same time, it is important for American students to learn other languages, experience foreign cultures, and develop a broad understanding of global issues. I am pleased that our new Gilman International Scholarship program will open study abroad opportunities to students with financial need, thus increasing both the number and diversity of participants in international exchanges.

International education prepares our citizens to live, work, and compete in the global economy, and promotes tolerance and the reduction of conflict. In November 2001 U.S. embassies around the world will carry out activities in support of International Education Week. I encourage schools, businesses, and communities to join with us in commemorating International Education Week.

FOREIGN LANGUAGES OFFERED AND AGE OF INTRODUCTION

Country	First Foreign	Starting Age	Compulsory*	Widely Available	Additional Foreign Languages
Australia	French	6		X	German, Greek, Italian, Japanese
Austria	English	6	X		French, Italian
Brazil	English	11 or 12	X		Spanish, French, German
Canada	French	10	X		German, Spanish, Italian, Japanese, Mandarin, Chinese, Punjabi
Chile	English	>12	?		French, German, Italian
Czech Republic	English and German	9	2X		French, Russian, Spanish
Denmark	English		10	2X	German, French, Spanish
Finland	English or other	9	2X		Swedish, Finnish, German, French, Russian, Spanish, Italian
Germany	English or other	8	2X		French, Spanish, Russian, Italian, Turkish
Israel	English	10	X		German, French
Italy	English	8	X		French, German, Spanish, Russian
Kazakhstan	English	10	X		German, French
Luxembourg	German and French	6 and 7	2X		English, Italian, Spanish
Morocco	French	9	X		English, Spanish, German
Netherlands	English	10 or 11	2X		German, French
New Zealand	French	>12		X	Japanese, Maori, German, Spanish
Peru	English	>12	?		French, German
Spain	English	8	X		French, German, Italian, Portuguese
Thailand	English	6		X	French, German, Chinese, Japanese, Arabic
United States	Spanish	14		X	French, German, Japanese

*2X means that two languages are compulsory.

Reprinted with permission by the ERIC/CLL from "What the U.S. Can Learn from Other Countries"
The full report is available at [http://www.cal.org/ericcll/countries.html].

Interview Questions for Visitation/Analysis of FLES Programs

I. Interviews Questions for school districts with FLES programs

Name of District_____ Language(s)_____

Year started_____ Model (FLEX, FLES, Immersion)

Grade starting_____ Contact person_____

1-What are the reasons the district decided to implement foreign languages at the

    elementary school level (FLES)?

2-Did the district ever offer FLES in the past?

3-If so, why did it stop?

4-What are the goals of the program?

5-Does the school district have a mission statement? If so, what is it?

6-What obstacles were encountered in implementing the program?

7-How was the program initiated?

8-Was there a committee? If so, who was on it?

9-How often is the language taught in a week?

10-How long is each class session?

11-How was the language(s) offered chosen?

12-Who teaches the classes?

13-Is it treated as a special with a visiting specialist to the class? If not, how?

14-Are the teachers of the program certified to teach FLES?

15-Where did they get the certification?

16-Are the FLES teachers scheduled to teach full-time? Part time?

17-From where was the time allowed for the instruction of the foreign language taken in the school day?

18-What are the reactions of the classroom teachers involved?

19-Are the FLES teachers using content-based instruction (teaching elementary curricula in the target language)?

20-What are the reactions of administrators in the district?

21-What are the reactions of parents?

22-What are the reactions of students?

23-What are the reactions of other foreign language teachers in the district?

24-Is the program being evaluated on an on-going basis?

25-Are the students being evaluated in any formal way?

26-Are there articulation plans with the middle/junior high school and high school?

27-What is the cost of the program? Breakdown:

Staffing—# of teachers: Staff development:

            students: Curriculum:

  elementary schools: Materials:

28-From where did the funding come for the program?

29-Was curriculum developed for the program? If so, by whom?

30-What are other current challenges to the program?

K-12 Performance Outcomes,
American Council of Teachers of Foreign Languages

NOVICE LEARNER RANGE
Grade K-4 or Grade 5-8 or Grade 9-10

COMPREHENSIBILITY: How well are they understood?

Interpersonal
- rely primarily on memorized phrases and short sentences during highly predictable interactions on very familiar topics;
- are understood primarily by those very accustomed to interacting with language learners;
- imitate modeled words and phrases using intonation and pronunciation similar to that of the model;
- may show evidence of false starts, prolonged and unexpectedly-placed pauses and recourse to their native language as topics expand beyond the scope of immediate needs;
- are able to meet limited practical writing needs, such as short messages and notes, by recombining learned vocabulary and structures to form simple sentences on very familiar topics.

Presentational
- use short, memorized phrases and sentences in oral and written presentations;
- are understood primarily by those who are very accustomed to interacting with language learners;
- demonstrate some accuracy in pronunciation and intonation when presenting well-rehearsed material on familiar topics;
- may show evidence of false starts, prolonged and unexpectedly-placed pauses, and recourse to their native language as topics expand beyond the scope of immediate needs;
- show abilities in writing by reproducing familiar material;
- rely heavily on visuals to enhance comprehensibility in both oral and written presentations.

COMPREHENSION: How well do they understand?

Interpersonal
- comprehend general information and vocabulary when the communication partner uses objects, visuals, and gestures in speaking or writing;
- generally need contextual clues, redundancy, paraphrase or restatement in order to understand the message.

Interpretive
- understand short, simple conversations and narratives (live or recorded material), within highly predictable and familiar contexts;
- rely on personal background experience to assist in comprehension;
- exhibit increased comprehension when constructing meaning through recognition of key words or phrases embedded in familiar contexts;
- comprehend written and spoken language better when content has been previously presented in an oral and/or visual context;
- determine meaning by recognition of cognates, prefixes, and thematic vocabulary.

CULTURAL AWARENESS: How is their cultural understanding reflected in their communication?

Interpersonal
- imitate culturally appropriate vocabulary and idiomatic expressions;
- use gestures and body language that are generally those of the student's own culture, unless they are incorporated into memorized responses.

Interpretive
- understand both oral and written language that reflects a cultural background similar to their own;
- predict a story line or event when it reflects a cultural background similar to their own.

Presentational
- imitate the use of culturally appropriate vocabulary, idiomatic expressions and non-verbal behaviors modeled by the teacher.

LANGUAGE CONTROL: How accurate is their language?

Interpersonal
- comprehend messages that include predominantly familiar grammatical structures;
- are most accurate when communicating about very familiar topics using memorized oral and written phrases;
- exhibit decreased accuracy when attempting to create with the language;
- write with accuracy when copying written language but may use invented spelling when writing words or producing characters on their own;
- may exhibit frequent errors in capitalization and/or punctuation when target language differs from native language in these areas.

Interpretive
- recognize structural patterns in target language narratives and derive meaning from these structures within familiar contexts;
- sometimes recognize previously learned structures when presented in new contexts.

Presentational
- demonstrate some accuracy in oral and written presentations when reproducing memorized words, phrases and sentences in the target language;
- formulate oral and written presentations using a limited range of simple phrases and expressions based on very familiar topics;
- show inaccuracies and/or interference from the native language when attempting to communicate information which goes beyond the memorized or pre-fabricated;
- may exhibit frequent errors in capitalization and/or punctuation and/or production of characters when the writing system of the target language differs from the native language.

VOCABULARY USE: How extensive and applicable is their vocabulary?

Interpersonal
- comprehend and produce vocabulary that is related to everyday objects and actions on a limited number of familiar topics;
- use words and phrases primarily as lexical items without awareness of grammatical structure;
- recognize and use vocabulary from a variety of topics including those related to other curricular areas;
- may often rely on words and phrases from their native language when attempting to communicate beyond the word and/or gesture level.

Interpretive
- recognize a variety of vocabulary words and expressions related to familiar topics embedded within relevant curricular areas;
- demonstrate increased comprehension of vocabulary in spoken passages when these are enhanced by pantomime, props, and/or visuals;
- demonstrate increased comprehension of written passages when accompanied by illustrations and other contextual clues.

Presentational
- use a limited number of words and phrases for common objects and actions in familiar categories;
- supplement their basic vocabulary with expressions acquired from sources such as the teacher or picture dictionaries;
- rely on native language words and phrases when expressing personal meaning in less familiar categories.

COMMUNICATION STRATEGIES: How do they maintain communication?

Interpersonal
- attempt to clarify meaning by repeating words and occasionally selecting substitute words to convey their message;
- primarily use facial expressions and gestures to indicate problems with comprehension.

Interpretive
- use background experience to anticipate story direction in highly predictable oral or written texts;
- rely heavily on visuals and familiar language to assist in comprehension.

Presentational
- make corrections by repeating or rewriting when appropriate forms are routinely modeled by the teacher;
- rely heavily on repetition, non-verbal expression (gestures, facial expressions), and visuals to communicate their message.

From "ACTFL K-12 Performance Guidelines." (1998). *Foreign Language Annals*, 31 (4), 484. (Reprinted with permission).

Appendix G

Syllabus: __Institute for the Certification of the Instruction of__
__Foreign Languages at the Elementary School Level (FLES)__

Dates and Times: Dowling College
Monday – Friday (8:30 am - 5:30 pm)   **Including 3 hours of Practicum
Instructor: Dr. Elaine Margarita   email: etmrpb@yahoo.com

This 45-hour institute will address the needs of certified secondary teachers of foreign languages interested in extending their certification to include the instruction of foreign languages at grades K-6. It will be offered through the Dowling Institute at Dowling College. The New York State Department of Education will grant certification upon completion of the 45 hours and submitting appropriate applications and fees.

__Course Objectives—For participants to be:__

1-familiar with FLES program models (FLEX, FLES, and Immersion) and the history of foreign language instruction at the elementary level.

2-able to write a proposal for a FLES program based on research, practice, and literature.

3-able to apply theories of second language acquisition and child development to the instruction of elementary aged children.

4-able to design activities, lesson plans, thematic units, and assessments for all elementary grade levels.

5-familiar with elementary level curricula in order to employ content-related instruction.

6-aware of a variety of methods for integrating culture into the FLES experience.

7-knowledgeable regarding current instructional materials available from various sources (publishing companies, teacher-made, etc.) suitable for use at the elementary level.

8-aware of the professional organizations and support networks in existence for teachers of FLES.

Class Meeting and Topic Schedule:

Day 1: Definitions and History of FLES. Readings=Curtain & Pesola, Lipton, Margarita.

Group work on program description.

Research and Rationales for FLES. Readings=Lipton, Margarita.

Groups=write a proposal for a FLES program.

Second Language Acquisition and the Characteristics of the Elementary-

Aged Learner. Readings=Curtain & Pesola, Heining-Boynton, Nork, Margarita.

Groups=profile of students at three levels.

Day 2: *Interviewing Elementary Aged Children. Groups work with visiting

children. Activities for FLES classes. Readings=Curtain & Pesola, Lipton.

Groups=preparing/sharing of activities for different elementary age groups.

Day 3: Content-related instruction and Thematic Units. Readings=Curtain (ERIC

Digest), Curtain & Pesola, Pesola (Dissertation). Groups=work on thematic units.

The Elementary Curriculum. Readings=Elementary Curriculum for Various School

Districts. Groups=preparing/sharing of Units.

Lesson Plans for FLES classes. Readings=Curtain & Pesola, Lipton, Nork, Margarita.

Groups=preparing/sharing of lessons.

Day 4: *Practicum with visiting students.

Culture in the FLES classroom. Summary of methods/approaches.

Readings=Curtain & Pesola, Lipton. Groups=pros and cons of approaches.

*Guest Speaker: To be arranged.

Day 5: FLES Assessment.   Readings=Curtain & Pesola, Lipton, Margarita.

Groups=preparing/sharing of assessment techniques.

FLES materials and professional support networks. Readings=Curtain & Pesola, Lipton,

Margarita. Groups=selection of items from catalogues.

Assignments/Group Activities:

The institute will be run as a participatory course with work done primarily in groups.

Attendance is required in order to meet eligibility for state certification.

Groups will read, discuss and write reactions to literature presented in class,

in addition to preparing assignments.

Each participant (in each group) will prepare:

1) A Proposal for a FLES program based on research

2) A Profile of elementary school aged children

3) A Lesson Plan to be used during the practicum with visiting elementary-aged

   children

4) A Thematic (Content-Related) Unit

5) An Assessment Technique for lesson presented

Evaluation:

The course is a P/F grade, based on:

1) full attendance

2) completion of assignments (individual work required during groups)

3) participation in practicum

Description of Assignments:

1) In your group, write a proposal for a FLES program in your school district. The proposal should include 8 parts: (1) a statement of philosophy, (2) a description of the program, (3) a rationale based on research, (4) program goals, (5) a description of the model (schedule, grades, etc.), (5) a cost analysis (staffing, staff development, materials, supplies, etc.), (6) curriculum and materials, (7) assessment and evaluation, (8) a discussion of the obstacles to the program and how they will be addressed. Each person in the group should write two of the eight sections. All group members should have a copy of the final proposal.

2) Groups will write a profile of a fictitious (or a real) elementary-aged children at various stages of development. The profile should include reference to theory on child development and should relate to educational experiences.

3) In your group, write a lesson plan for a selected grade level. The lesson should reflect your awareness of the developmental stage of the students. It should include visuals, small group or paired activities and culturally relevant material. Using the models of lesson plans provided, include the:

*grade level

*learning objective(s)

*demonstration of communicative orientation (language function)

*materials and visuals

*cultural component

*vocabulary and/or structures included

*detailed description of each activity

4) In your group, write a thematic (or content-related) unit based on a topic from the elementary curricula provided. Keep in mind the:

-language skills necessary to deal with content

-opportunities for language development

-potential for advancement of theme

-potential for integration with cultural information

-developmental appropriateness of content and tasks

-meaningfulness and interest value for students (Curtain & Pesola, 1994, p. 161).

Using the models provided, include:

*the thematic center

*the outcomes for language in use, content and culture

*materials

*classroom setting

*activities (at least five)

*ideas for assessment strategies (Pesola, 1995)

5) In your group, write an assessment technique for the lesson or the thematic unit you have prepared. Demonstrate that the evaluation:

-is contextualized and meaningful

-uses clearly defined rubrics (performance assessment)

-is an opportunity for the children to discover how much they know, not how

 much they still have to learn

-tests what has been taught in the way it has been taught

(Curtain & Pesola, 1994, pp. 222-227)

Required Texts:

Curtain, H., & Pesola, C. (1994). *Languages and children: Making the match. foreign language instruction for an early start, grades K-8.* White Plains, New York: Longman.

Lipton, G. (1998). *Practical handbook to elementary foreign language programs. including FLES, FLEX, and immersion programs* (3rd ed.). Lincolnwood, Illinois: National Textbook Company.

References:

Curtain, H., & Haas, M. (1995). *Integrating foreign language and content instruction in grades K-8.* (Report No. EDO-FL-95-07). Washington, DC: ERIC Clearinghouse on Languages and Linguistics. (ERIC Document Reproduction Service No. ED 381 018)

Heining-Boynton, D. (1991). The developing child: What every FLES teacher needs to know. In L. Strasheim (Ed.), *Central States Conference on the Teaching of Foreign Languages: Focus on the foreign language learner: Priorities and strategies* (pp. 3-11). Lincolnwood, IL: National Textbook Company.

Margarita, E. (1999). *Implementing Foreign Languages at the Elementary School Level (FLES).* Dissertation Abstracts, Hofstra University.

Nork, L. (1994). Foreign language in the elementary school: Focusing on higher order thinking skills. (Masters Thesis, Eastern Michigan University, 1994). *Masters Abstracts International, 33/03,* 727.

Pesola, C. (1995). Background, design and evaluation of a conceptual framework for FLES curriculum (Doctoral Dissertation, University of Minnesota, 1995). *Dissertation Abstracts International, A 56/12,* 4653.

Appendix H

Federal or State Funding and Other Resources

1. The Fund for the Improvement of Post secondary Education (FIPSE) offers a yearly grant through the National K-12 Foreign Language Resource Center. United States Department of Education Office of Post Secondary Education Fund for the Improvement of Post Secondary Education, Regional Office Building 3, Seventh and D Streets SW, Washington, DC 20202, (202) 708-5750 (www.ed.gov/offices/OPE/FIPSE)

2. National Endowment for the Humanities, Grants, Division of Research and Education Public Information Office Room 402, 1100 Pennsylvania Avenue NW, Washington, DC 20506, (202) 606-8400 (www.neh.gov)

3. United States Department of Education Office of Bilingual Education and Minority Languages Affairs Foreign Language Assistance Program (FLAP) 330 C Street SW Fifth floor, Washington, DC 20202-6510, (202) 205-9808 (www.ed.gov/offices/OBEMLA)

4. Joint National Committee on Languages-NCLIS 4646 40th St. NW, Suite 310 Washington, DC 20026-1859, (202) 966-8477 (www. info@languagepolicy.org)

5. National K-12 Foreign Language Resource Center, N157 Lagomarcion Hall Iowa State University, Ames, IA 50011, (515) 294-6699 (www.educ.iastate.edu)

Note: See also; Boston, C. (1998). *ERIC Review, K-12 Foreign Language Education, 6* (1), pp. 42-43.

Appendix I

Content-Based Bibliography Prepared by, Audrey L. Heining-Boynton, 10/1/98

Allison, Linda. *Blood & Guts: A Working Guide to Your Own Insides.* Little, Brown and Co. ISBN # 0-316-03443-6

Anderson, Karen C. *Kid's Big Book of Games.* Workman Publishing Company, 1987. ISBN # 0-89480-657-2

Anderson, Karen C. *Kid's Giant Book of Games.* B. &P. Publishing Company, Inc., 1993. ISBN # 0-8129-2199-2

Anderson, Karen C., and Cumbaa, Stephen. *The Bones and Skeleton Game Book.* Workman Publishing Company, 1993. ISBN # 1-56305-497-3

Beakman's World Calendar. ISBN # 0-8362-7270-6

Beaumont, Emile. *Dinosaurios.* Sasaeta Ediciones, S.A., 1991. ISBN # 8-305-725-6

Benton Michael. *Dinosaur and Other Prehistoric Animal Fact Finder.* Grisewood & Dempsey, Inc., ISBN # 1-85697-802-8

Bittinger, Gayle. *Exploring Water and the Ocean.* Warren Publishing House, 1993. ISBN # 0-911019-59-6

Booth, Jerry. *The Big Beast Book.* The Yolla Bolly Press, 1988. ISBN # 0-316-10266-0

Brinton, Donna M.; Snow, Marguerite Ann; and Wesche; Marjorie Gingham. *Content-Based Second Language Instruction.* Heinle & Heinle Publishers, 1989. ISBN#0-8384-2677-8

Heining-Boynton Bibliography

Brown, Robert J. *Science For You, 112 Illustrated Experiments.* Tab Books Inc.,

1988. ISBN # 0-8306-9325-4

Brown, Robert J. *200 Illustrated Science Experiments for Children.* Tab Books, Inc.,

1987. ISBN # 0-8306-2825-8

Burns, Marilyn. *The I Hate Mathematics! Book.* Little Brown and Co.

ISBN # 0-316-11741-2

Cantoni-Harvey, Gina. *Content-Area Language Instruction: Approaches and*

Strategies. Addison-Wesley Publishing Company, 1987. ISBN # 0-201-14097-7

Caroll, Susan. *How Big Is A Brachiosaurus?* Platt & Munk, Publishers, 1986.

ISBN # 0-418-19077-X

Cash, Terry; Parker, Steve; and Taylor, Barbara, 175 *More Science Experiments*

to Amuse and Amaze Your Friends. Random House,1989. ISBN # 0-679-80390-4

Cauley, Lorinda Bryan. *The Trouble with Tyrannosaurus Rex.* Harcourt Brace

Jovanovich, 1988. ISBN # 0-15-290880-3

Cobb, Vicki. *Science Experiments You Can Eat.* J.P. Lippincott Company, 1972.

ISBN # 0-397-31253-9

Cornell, Joseph. *Sharing Nature with Children.* Dawn Publications, 1979.

ISBN # 0-916124-14-2

Cornell, Joseph. *Sharing the Joy of Nature.* Dawn Publications, 1989.

ISBN # 0-91612-52-5

Heining-Boynton Bibliography

The Visual Dictionary of Dinosaurs. Dorling Kindersley, Inc., 1993.

ISBN # 1-56458-188-8

Earth Works Group. *50 Simple Things You Can Do To Save The Earth.* Earth Works

Press, 1989. ISBN # 0-929634-06-3

¡En español! Levels 1, 2, and 3. McDougal Littell, 1999. (800) 323-5435

www. mcdougallittell.com

Elting, Mary. *Dinosaurs.* Western Publishing Company, Inc., 1987.

ISBN # 0-307-11912-2

Griffiths, Rachel, and Clyne, Margaret. *Books You Can Count On.* Heinemann, 1991.

ISBN # 0-435-08322-8

Hart-Davis, Adam. *Scientific Eye.* Sterling Publishing Company, Inc., 1989.

ISBN # 0-8069-5758-1

Heining-Boynton, Audrey L. & Sonia Torres-Quiñones. *¡Animate! Focus on*

Science and Math. Introductory Spanish. Addison-Wesley Publishing, 1996: White

Plains, N.Y. ISBN # 0-8013-1601-4

Heining-Boynton, Audrey L. & Sonia Torres-Quiñones. *¡Animate! Focus on*

Science and Math. Introductory Spanish. Teacher's Guide. Addison-Wesley

Publishing, 1996; White Plains, N.Y. ISBN # 0-8013-1602-2

Herbert, Don. *Mr. Wizard's Supermarket Science.* Random House, Inc., 1980.

ISBN # 0-394-83800-9

Heining-Boynton Bibliography

Jacobs, Heidi Hayes. *Interdisciplinary Curriculum: Design and Implementation.*

Association for Supervision and Curriculum Development, 1989.

ISBN # 0-87120-165-8

Keegan, Thomas. 175 *Amazing Nature Experiments.* Random House, 1991.

ISBN # 0-679-82043-4

Kenda, Margaret, and Williams, Phyllis S. *Science Wizardry for Kids.* Barron's

Educational Series, Inc., 1992. ISBN # 0-8120-1809-5

Kenda, Margaret, and Williams, Phyllis S. *Math Wizardry for Kids.* Barron's

Educational Series, Inc., 1995. ISBN # 0-8120-4766-4

Kricher, John. *A Field Guide to Tropical Forests Coloring Book.* Houghton Mifflin

Company, 1991. ISBN # 0-395-57321-1

Lambert, David. *The Age of Dinosaurs.* Random House. ISBN # 0-394-88975-4

Mandell, Muriel. *Simple Science Experiments With Everyday Materials.* Sterling

Publishing Company, Inc., 1989. ISBN # 0-8069-6794-3

Massey, Sue J., and Darst, Diane W. *Learning to Look.* Prentice Hall Professional

Publishing, 1992. ISBN # 0-13-528795-2

McLoone-Basta & Alice Siegel. *The Second Kids' World Almanac.* World Almanac:

New York, 1987. ISBN # 0-88687-317-7

National Gallery of Art. *Nature in Art Quiz.* Washington. An Educational Game.

Newman, Arnold. *Tropical Rainforest.* Facts On File, 1990. ISBN # 0-8160-1911-1

Norman, David, and Milner, Angela. *Los Dinosaurios.* Toppan Printing Company, 1993.

ISBN # 84-372-3720-3

Petreshene, Susan S. *Brain Teasers!* The Center for Applied Research in Education, Inc.,

1994. ISBN # 0-87628-123-4

Petreshene, Susan S. *Mind Joggers!* The Center for Applied Research in Education, Inc.,

1985. ISBN # 0-87628-583-3

Prochnow, Dave & Kathy Prochnow. *Why? Experiments for the young scientist.* TAB

Books. 1993. ISBN # 0-8306-4023-1

Quinn, Kaye. *Hidden Pictures Coloring Book.* Price Stern Sloan, Inc.

ISBN # 0-8431-3385-6

Raboff, Ernest. *Pablo Picasso.* Ernest Raboff and Gemini-Smith, Inc., 1982.

ISBN # 0-385-17935-9

Robson, Pam. *Water/Paddles & Boats.* Shooting Star Press. ISBN # 1-56924-007-8

Robson, Pam. *Clocks/Scales & Measurements.* Shooting Star Press.

ISBN # 1-57335-151-2

Ruiz, José Curbelo; Hernandez, Maàia Teresa; and Zuazo, Prudencio. *La Ciencia*

*1.*SM Ediciones, 1985.   ISBN # 84-499-2450-2

Ruiz, José Curbelo; Hernandez, Maàia Teresa; and Zuazo, Prudencio. *La Ciencia*

2. SM Ediciones, ISBN # 84-499-2450-2

Ruiz, José Curbelo; Hernandez, Maàia Teresa; and Zuazo, Prudencio. *La Ciencia*

3. SM Ediciones, 1983. ISBN # 84-199-2819-2

Heining-Boynton Bibliography

Ruiz, José Curbelo; Hernandez, Maàia Teresa; and Zuazo, Prudencio. *La Ciencia 4.* SM Ediciones, 1979. ISBN # 81-499-2889-3

Ruiz, José Curbelo; Hernandez, Maàia Teresa; and Zuazo, Prudencio. *La Ceincia 5.* SM Ediciones, ISBN # 84-499-3504-0

Schmittberger, R. Wayne. *Big Book of Games II.* Workman Publishing Company Inc., 1979. ISBN # 0-89480-632-7

Schneider, Herman and Nina. *Quick Science.* Scholastic, Inc., 1975. ISBN # 0-590-41354-6

Seabury, Debra L. *Earth Smart: Ready-to-Use Environmental Science Activities for the Elementary Classroom.* The Center for Applied Research in Education, 1994. ISBN # 0-87628-306-7

Seabury, Debra L. and Peeples, Susan L. *Ready-to-Use Social Studies Activities for the Elementary Classroom.* The Center for Applied Research in Education, Inc., 1989. ISBN # 0-87628-788-7

Seager, Joni. *The State of the Earth Atlas.* Simon & Schuster, Inc., 1990. ISBN # 10-671-70524-5

Seller, Mick. *Elements/Mixtures & Reactions.* Shooting Star Press. ISBN #1-57335-328-0

Seller, Mick. *Sound/Noise & Music.* Shooting Star Press. ISBN # 57335-149-0

Spizzirri, Linda. *Ocean Life.* Spizzirri Publishing, Inc., 1992. ISBN # 0-86545216-4

Spurgeon, Richard. *Usborne Science & Experiments Ecology.* Usborne Publishing Ltd., 1988. ISBN # 0-7460-0287-4

Heining-Boynton Bibliography

Stand Up Math. Good Year Books

Stec, Ruth Ellen. *The Coloring-Activities Book of Endangered Species.* RMS

Publishing, 1992. ISBN # 0-9632284-0-4

Sterling, Mary Ellen. *Oceans.* Teacher Created Materials, Inc., 1990.

ISBN # 1-55734-284-9

Striker, Susan. *The Newspaper Anti-Coloring Book.* Henry Holt and Company,

Inc., 1992. ISBN # 0-8050-1599-X

Striker, Susan. *The Sixth Anti-Coloring Book.* Henry Holt and Company, Inc.,

1984. ISBN # 0-8050-0873-X

Striker, Susan, and Kimmel, Edward. *The Anti-Coloring Book.* Henry Holt and

Company, Inc., 1978. ISBN # 0-8050-0246-4

VanCleave, Janice Pratt. *Biology for Every Kid, 101 Easy Experiments that

Really Work.* John Wiley & Sons, Inc., 1990. ISBN # 0-471-50381-9

Van Cleave, Janice Pratt. *Chemistry for Every Kid, 101 Easy Experiments that

Really Work.* John Wiley & Sons, Inc., 1989. ISBN # 0-471-62085-8

Venzia, Mike. *Francisco Goya.* Children's Press, 1993. ISBN # 0-516-02292-X

Venzia, Mike. *Picasso.* Children's Press, 1988. ISBN # 0-516-02271-7

Walpole, Brenda, *175 Science Experiments to Amuse and Amaze Your Friends.*

Random House, 1988. ISBN # 0-394-89991-1

Webster, Vera R. *Experimentos Atmosféricos.* Regensteiner Publishing

Enterprises, Inc., 1982. ISBN # 0-516-31662-1

Heining-Boynton Bibliography

West, David. *Brain Surgery for Beginners and Other Major Operations for Minors.*
The Millbrook Press. ISBN # 1-56294-895-4

Wiebe, Ann; Bezerra-Nader, Rosemarie; Highlund, Susan B.; Cohrs, Merriellen;
Lusk, Susan F.; Davies, Julie Ann; Wahab, Scot; and Waltner, Doug. *Finding
Your Bearings.* AIMS Education Foundation, 1990. ISBN # 0-881431-26-6

Willow, Diane, and Jacques, Laura. *At Home in the Rainforest.* Charlesbridge,
1991. ISBN # 0-88106-485-8

Winter, Stephen S., and Caruso, Joseph. *Spanish Math Terms.* J. Weston
Walch, 1993. ISBN # 0-8251-2285-6

Wollard, Kathy. *How Come?* Workman Publishing Company, Inc., 1993.
ISBN # 1-56305-324-1

Wright, Alexandra. *¿Les echaremos de menos? Especies en peligro de extinción.*
Charlesbridge Publishing, 1993. ISBN # 0-88106-420-3

Zallinger, Peter. *Dinosaurs.* Random House, 1977. ISBN # 0-394-83445-3

Sample Report Cards for a FLES Program

Sample 1

Foreign Language	Shows Effort	Good	Very Good
Oral Participation			
Listening Skills			
Reading or Writing Tasks			
Cultural Awareness			

Sample 2

Grading Code: 1=Excellent 2=Very Good 3=Good 4=Satisfactory 5=Needs Improvement				
Foreign Language	Fall	Winter	Spring	Summer
Linguistic Achievement				
Class Participation				
Cooperation				
Effort				

Sample 3

4 Often	3 Sometimes	2 Rarely	1 Never

Participation   _____

Effort   _____

Demonstrates Appreciation of or
Interest in Target Language and Culture   _____

Appendix K

Sample Instrument for Program Evaluation

FLES PROGRAM EVALUATION INVENTORY

FOR FLES TEACHERS

By Audrey L. Heining-Boynton, University of North Carolina at Chapel Hill

Please answer the following questionnaire concerning the **Foreign Language in the Elementary School (FLES)** program in your school. Please return this survey in the envelope provided no later than one week after receipt. Your opinion is important. All responses are anonymous.

After reading each statement carefully, circle the one response that best represents your own opinion. The abbreviated coding is: STRONGLY AGREE = SA; AGREE = A; DISAGREE = D; STRONGLY DISAGREE = SD; NO ANSWER/NOT APPLICABLE = NA.

1. I am aware of the goals and objectives of our FLES program.

      SA   A   D   SD   NA

2. The goals and objectives of our FLES program are realistic.

      SA   A   D   SD   NA

3. The students have achieved the objectives of the FLES program for this year.

      SA   A   D   SD   NA

4. Our FLES philosophy is written and available for all interested parties.

      SA   A   D   SD   NA

5. My FLES students receive a foreign language grade on their report

   card.

           SA   A   D   SD   NA

6. When appropriate, I assign my students homework.

           SA   A   D   SD   NA

7. My "at-risk" students are doing well.

           SA   A   D   SD   NA

8. I get along with the regular classroom teachers.

           SA   A   D   SD   NA

9. The principal(s) of my building(s) are supportive.

           SA   A   D   SD   NA

10. The parents of my students are supportive.

            SA   A   D   SD   NA

11. The FLES coordinator (if one exists) is supportive of the program.

            SA   A   D   SD   NA

12. Opportunities are provided to network with other colleagues.

            SA   A   D   SD   NA

13. In-service programs are provided.

            SA   A   D   SD   NA

14. The in-service programs are informative and useful for my job.

            SA   A   D   SD   NA

15. Sufficient resources are available to allow me to adequately do my job.

            SA   A   D   SD   NA

16. Time is provided to work on materials.

        SA   A   D   SD   NA

17. My teaching load is reasonable.

        SA   A   S   SD   NA

18. I feel good about my FLES teaching.

        SA   A   S   SD   NA

19. My job is rewarding to me.

        SA   A   S   SD   NA

ADDITIONAL COMMENTS: If you feel this questionnaire did not allow you to adequately express your opinion, or if you care to elaborate on a point(s), please no so on the back of this sheet.

THANK YOU FOR YOUR TIME, INPUT, AND COOPERATION.

FLES PROGRAM

EVALUATION INVENTORY

FOR PRINCIPALS AND ADMINISTRATORS

By Audrey L. Heining-Boynton, University of North Carolina at Chapel Hill

Please answer the following questionnaire concerning the **Foreign Language in the Elementary School (FLES)** program in your school. Please return this survey in the envelope provided no later than one week after receipt. Your opinion is important. All responses are anonymous.

After reading each statement carefully, circle the one response that best represents your own opinion. The abbreviated coding is: STRONGLY AGREE = SA; AGREE = A; DISAGREE = D; STRONGLY DISAGREE = SD; NO ANSWER/NOT APPLICABLE = NA.

1. I have personally observed the FLES teacher in my building.

    SA   A   D   SD   NA

2. The FLES teacher is liked by the other teachers in my building.

    SA   A   D   SD   NA

3. The FLES program is liked by the other teachers in the building.

    SA   A   D   SD   NA

4. The parents seem pleased with the FLES program.

    SA   A   D   SD   NA

5. The students seem pleased with the FLES program.

    SA   A   D   SD   NA

6. The students participate enthusiastically.

        SA   A   D   SD   NA

7. The "at-risk" students are performing well in the foreign language classroom.

        SA   A   D   SD   NA

8. The FLES class is organized.

        SA   A   D   SD   NA

9. The FLES teacher is enthusiastic.

        SA   A   D   SD   NA

10. The FLES lessons are interesting and age-appropriate.

        SA   A   D   SD   NA

11. The study of foreign language is reinforcing the other content areas of the curriculum.

        SA   A   D   SD   NA

12. I support the notion that foreign language is important for all students.

        SA   A   D   SD   NA

ADDITIONAL COMMENTS: If you feel this questionnaire did not allow you to adequately express your opinion, or if you care to elaborate on a point(s), please no so on the back of this sheet.

THANK YOU FOR YOUR TIME, INPUT, AND COOPERATION.

FLES PROGRAM

EVALUATION INVENTORY

FOR CLASSROOM TEACHERS

By Audrey L. Heining-Boynton, University of North Carolina at Chapel Hill

Please answer the following questionnaire concerning the **Foreign Language in the Elementary School (FLES)** program in your school. Please return this survey in the envelope provided no later than one week after receipt. Your opinion is important. All responses are anonymous.

After reading each statement carefully, circle the one response that best represents your own opinion. The abbreviated coding is: STRONGLY AGREE = SA; AGREE = A; DISAGREE = D; STRONGLY DISAGREE = SD; NO ANSWER/NOT APPLICABLE = NA.

1. The students are enjoying the foreign language instruction.

    SA   A   D   SD   NA

2. The students appear to be learning the foreign language.

    SA   A   D   SD   NA

3. The FLES teacher has the students actively involved in language learning.

    SA   A   D   SD   NA

4. The FLES teacher keeps the students on task.

    SA   A   D   SD   NA

5. The foreign language lessons are organized.

    SA   A   D   SD   NA

6. The foreign language teacher is knowledgeable in his/her field.

SA   A   D   SD   NA

7. The foreign language activities are at the appropriate age level for the child.

SA   A   D   SD   NA

8. The foreign language teacher is enthusiastic.

SA   A   D   SD   NA

9. The foreign language class is lively and varied in activities.

SA   A   D   SD   NA

10. The foreign language is the main language of instruction.

SA   A   D   SD   NA

11. The foreign language curriculum enhances and reinforces the regular curriculum.

SA   A   D   SD   NA

12. I agree with the methodology used to teach foreign language to elementary students.

SA   A   D   SD   NA

13. The FLES teacher is courteous, friendly, and polite toward the regular classroom teacher.

SA   A   D   SD   NA

14. There is communication between the foreign language teacher and the regular classroom teacher.

SA   A   D   SD   NA

15. I understand the goals or expectations of our FLES program.

    SA   A   D   SD   NA

16. I am well informed about our FLES program, its goals and techniques.

    SA   A   D   SD   NA

ADDITIONAL COMMENTS: If you feel this questionnaire did not allow you to

adequately express your opinion, or if you care to elaborate on a point(s), please no so on

the back of this sheet.

THANK YOU FOR YOUR TIME, INPUT, AND COOPERATION.

FLES PROGRAM

EVALUATION INVENTORY

FOR CHILDREN (GRADES K-2)

By Audrey L. Heining-Boynton, University of North Carolina at Chapel Hill

DIRECTIONS FOR THE CLASSROOM TEACHER

Hand out one evaluation form to each child. Read the following questions, and ask the children to circle on their paper the happy face if they answer "yes", the frowning face if they answer "no" to the question. All responses are anonymous. Please return the forms in the envelope provided to the foreign language teacher. Thank you for your cooperation.

1. Do you like your (Spanish, French, etc.) class?

2. Do you like your (Spanish, French, etc.) teacher?

3. Is (Spanish, French, etc.) fun?

4. Do you want to learn more (Spanish, French, etc.)?

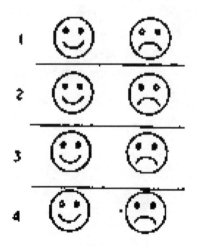

FLES PROGRAM

EVALUATION INVENTORY

FOR PARENTS

By Audrey L. Heining-Boynton, University of North Carolina at Chapel Hill

Please answer the following questionnaire concerning the **Foreign Language in the Elementary School (FLES)** program in your school. Please return this survey in the envelope provided no later than one week after receipt. Your opinion is important. All responses are anonymous.

After reading each statement carefully, circle the one response that best represents your own opinion. The abbreviated coding is: STRONGLY AGREE = SA; AGREE = A; DISAGREE = D; STRONGLY DISAGREE = SD; NO ANSWER/ NOT APPLICABLE = NA.

1. My child talks at home about foreign language class.

> SA   A   D   SD   NA

2. My child's comments are positive about foreign language learning.

> SA   A   D   SD   NA

3. My child feels successful in the foreign language class.

> SA   A   D   SD   NA

4. My child likes the foreign language.

> SA   A   D   SD   NA

5. My child likes the foreign language teacher.

> SA   A   D   SD   NA

6. I am receiving enough information about the foreign language program at our elementary school.

   SA A   D   SD NA

7. I have seen my child participating in a foreign language school program.

   SA A   D   SD NA

8. I have visited my child's foreign language classroom.

   SA A   D   SD NA

9. My child brings home foreign language worksheets, song handouts, etc. that I feel are helpful.

   SA A   D   SD NA

10. My child uses the foreign language or talks about the foreign language class at home.

   SA A   D   SD NA

11. I am in favor of teaching a foreign language to children.

   SA A   D   SD NA

12. I feel that studying foreign language has not jeopardized my child's progress in the other subject areas such as math or reading.

   SA A   D   SD NA

13. ANSWER THIS QUESTION ONLY IF YOUR CHILD HAS BEEN DESIGNATED AS AN "AT RISK" STUDENT OR IS LEARNING DISABLED.

My child is benefiting from the elementary foreign language program at our elementary school.

SA   A   D   SD   NA

ADDITIONAL COMMENTS: If you feel this questionnaire did not allow you to adequately express your opinion, or if you care to elaborate on a point(s), please no so on the back of this sheet.

THANK YOU FOR YOUR TIME, INPUT, AND COOPERATION.

Heining-Boynton, A. (1991). The FLES Program Evaluation Inventory (FPEI).

Foreign Language Annals 24 (3), 193-202. Reprinted with permission.

Sample FLES Newsletter

Inside this Newsletter (Prepared by Eglal Nasser, Syosset Schools)

1. The song "Sur le Pont d'Avigon"

2. The comptine "Il pleut, il mouille..."

3. Recipe for the Tarte Tatin

4. Did you know?

5. Counting from 0 to 10.

6. The puppets Gribouille and Lucien.

Sur le Pont d'Avigon.

On the Bridge at Avigon

Avigon is a town in Provence, in the south of France. There is a bridge across the Rhône River that was built hundreds of years ago. Only half of it is left now. There is a French song about the bridge. There are some actions for the second part of the song. The following are the words to the song:

Sur le pont d'Avigon On y danse, on y danse. Sur le pont d'Avignon on y danse tout en rond. Les garçons font comme ça (the boys bow.) Et les filles font comme ça (all the girls curtsy).

On the Bridge of Avigon, we dance, we dance. On the bridge we dance in a circle. The boys do like this (the boys bow), and the girls do like this (all the girls curtsy).

Il Pleut, il mouille

C'est le fête de la grenouille

Quand il ne pleuvra plus

Ce sera le fête de la tortue.

It rains, it's wet.

The frog is partying.

When it will not rain,

it will be the party of the turtle.

La pomme.

With Madame Nasser we examined an apple. We learned the different parts in French. La peau, la chair, et les pépins, (which means, the skin, the inside of the apple, and the seeds). We were given a grid and we had to draw the apple in the first box, then take a bite, and draw the apple after the first bite, take another bite, then draw the apple again, and eat until the 12 boxes of the grid were filled. We also learned the products derived from the apple, such as le jus de pomme, le cidre, les croustilles, la Tarte Tatin, les bonbons, et la compote. (Which means apple juice, cider, apple chips, apple pie, candies, and stewed apples.)

Tarte Tatin

Upside-Down Apple Tart

This famous French tart is named after the young ladies Tatin, who owned a restaurant in Sologne at the beginning of this century called 'Le Motte-Beuvron.' It was first served in Paris at Maxim's, where it remains a specialty to this day.

1/2 cup softened butter

2 1/2 lb. small crisp dessert apples

1/2 lb. pâte brisée

For the pâte brisée (basic pie dough)*

2 cups all-purpose flour

1/2 teaspoon salt

1/2 cup butter

about 1/4 cup iced water

Brush the base of a 9 to 10 inch round flameproof baking dish with two thirds of the butter. Sprinkle with two thirds of the sugar. Peel, halve, and core the apples. Arrange the apple halves in the dish, cut sides facing upwards and pressing them firmly together. (It does not matter if they come above the edge of the dish - they will shrink down during cooking.) Sprinkle with the remaining sugar, then dot with the remaining butter. Cook the apples over moderate heat for about 20 minutes until they begin to caramelize underneath. Transfer to a preheated moderately hot oven (400F) and bake for about 5 minutes until the apples become caramelized on top. Remove from the oven and set aside. Roll out the dough thinly on a floured surface to a circle large enough to cover the baking dish. Place the pastry over the dish, then trim around the edge with a knife so that the pastry falls inside the dish to enclose the apples. Return the dish to the hot oven and bake for another 20 minutes or until the pastry is crisp and golden. Remove from the oven and immediately invert the dish onto a serving platter. Leave to cool slightly. Serve warm. Serves 6.

*Pâte Brisée

Basic pie dough

Sift the flour and salt into a bowl. Cut the butter into small pieces over the bowl then, with a round-bladed knife, cut it into the flour. With the fingertips, rub the butter into the flour until the mixture resembles fine breadcrumbs. Work lightly, with hands held above the rim of the bowl to aerate the flour as much as possible to keep it light and short. Stir in the water with the knife, adding it gradually until the mixture begins to draw together. With one hand, gather the dough together and form into a ball. Knead lightly until the dough is smooth and supple and free from cracks. Wrap in cling film or foil, then leave to relax in a cool place for 1 hour before use. In warm weather, chill in the refrigerator for 30 minutes, but allow to come to room temperature again before rolling out.

Makes a 1/2 lb. quantity.

Did You Know?

Normandy! Land of apple orchards. A land of rich culinary tradition based on its wealth of fine local produce: the world's prestigious Calvados! Calvados is a brandy made by distilling cider. Calvados is a harsh rough brandy, 72 degree, which must mature for a time in oak casks. It may only be sold after a year's aging. It is usually categorized as follows: "Trois étoiles" or "Trois Pommes" Calavados are aged for two years in wood. "Vieux" or "Réserve" are aged for three years; "VO" (very old) or "Vieille Réserve" for four years; "VSOP" for five years; "Extra," "Napoléon," "Hors d'Age" or "Age Inconnu" for more than five years.

We now know how to count from 0 to 10.

zéro - un - deux - trois - quatre - cinq - six sept - huit - neuf - dix.

Meet our friends Gribouille and Lucien.

Les marionettes (The Puppets Gribouille and Lucien):

G. Bonjour! Je m'appelle Gribouille (Good morning! My name is Gribouille).

L.   Bonjour! Je m'appelle Lucien.

G. Tu es une fille? (Are you a girl?)

L.   Non!

G. Tu es un garçon? (Are you a boy?)

L.   Non! Non!

G.   Alors? (So?)

L.   Je suis un chien. Ouaf! Ouaf! (I am a dog! Ruff! Ruff!)

G. Ah!

L. Tu es une fille?

G. Non!

L.   Tu es un garçon?

G.   Non! Non!

L.   Alors?

G.   Je suis une grenouille! Croak, croak, croak (I am a frog! Ribitt! Ribitt!).

L.   Je m'appelle Lucien, je suis un

       chien. Ouaf! Ouaf! Ouaf!

G.   Je m'appelle Gribouille,

       je suis une grenouille. Croak! Croak! Croak!

G. & L. Et nous sommes des amis! (And we are friends!)

Appendix M

FLES Support Networks

There are a number of national, state, and local organizations that serve as FLES support

networks. These organizations, (1) advocate for FLES programs, (2) provide

opportunities for staff development, (3) provide access to research and discussion from

the field, (4) offer networking opportunities for employment, and (5) provide information

on materials, curriculum, and instructional techniques. Contact information is provided

wherever possible (also see Curtain & Pesola, 1994, pp. 393-400).

- AATG (American Association of Teachers of German) (609) 795-5553

- AATI (American Association of Teachers of Italian) (313) 577-3219

- AATC (American Association of Teachers of Arabic) 280 HRCB Brigham Young

  University Provo, UT 84602

- AATF (American Association of Teachers of French) Annual Reports of FLES*

  Commission 1000 Hilltop Circle Baltimore, MD 21250

- ACL (American Classical League) (513) 529-7741

- ACTFL (American Council of Teachers of Foreign Languages Foreign Language

  Annals) acftlhq@aol.com,http://www.actfl.org

- ACTR (American Council of Teachers of Russian) (202) 328-2287

- AATSP (American Association of Teachers of Spanish and Portuguese) University

  of North Colorado Gunter Hall Greeley, CO 80639

- ALL (Advocates for Language Learning) (816) 871-6317

- CAL (Center for Applies Linguistics) www.cal.org/earlylang

- CLTA (Chinese Language Teachers' Association) Kalamazoo College 1200 Academy Street Kalamazoo, MI 49006 (616) 383-5671

- ERIC/CLL Publications http://www.cal.org/ericcll/pubdescribe.html or www.accesseric.org,www.cal.org/ericcll/

- FLACS (Foreign Language Association of Chairpersons and Supervisors) http://schools.portnet.k12.ny.us/~flacs (remember not to use www)

- FLTeach (listserv: http://www.cortland.edu/www_root/teach/flteach.html)

- Japanese Teachers Network University High School, 1212 West Springfield Avenue, Urbana, IL 61801

- JNCL (Joint National Committee for Languages)/NCLIS (National Council for Languages and International Studies) (202) 966-8477 Email=76306.535@compuserve.com

- LILT (Long Island Language Teachers) www.liltfl.org

- MLA (Modern Language Association) 10 Astor Place, NY 10003, mla.org

- National K-12 Foreign Language Resource Center Email: nflrc@iastate.edu

- NFI (National FLES* Institute of the University of Maryland) (301) 231-0824, Email=lipton@umbc2.umbc.edu

- NNELL (National Network for Early Language Learning) www.cal.org/earlylang To join the listserv, send email message to: ñandu-request@caltalk.cal.org

- Northeast Conference on the Teaching of Foreign Languages (802) 862-9939

- SLAC (Second Language Acquisition by Children Conference) (405) 332-8000

- U.S. Gov http://www.gov.ed/opeagenda

- Brochures: http://www.cal.org, http://www.access/eric.org

Sample FLES Lesson Plans

Kindergarten Spanish Lesson
Prepared by Mary Jane McMaster, Southampton Schools

Objective

Students will be able to identify numbers 1-10 in the target language.

Length of Lesson   (20 minutes)

NYS STANDARDS:

A.   Students engage in conversations, provide and obtain information, express

feelings and emotions, and exchange opinions.

B.   Students understand and interpret written and spoken language on a variety of

topics.

C.   Students reinforce and further their knowledge of other disciplines through the

foreign language.

Materials

Cassette tape *Diez Deditos/Ten Little Fingers* by Jose Orozco, portable CD/cassette

sound system, the book *Somos Amigos* by Lada Josefa Kratky, song chart for *Diez*

Deditos, postal box covered with contact paper, large number cards 1-10.

Warm up   2 minutes

Students sing a greeting song *"Buenos Días".* Teacher will ask various students *¿Cómo*

estás? Students will respond *Estoy bien, Estoy mal, Estoy así, así.*

Activity 1 (5 minutes)

Teacher will read the book *Somos Amigos* by Lada Josefa Kratky. As teacher reads this big book, students will count the children on each page of the book.

Activity 2 (5 minutes)

Teacher will play the song *Diez Deditos* by Jose Orozco. Students will sing along, following the song chart and doing the finger play. See attached for song lyrics.

Activity 3 (5 minutes)

Play the Box Toss Game. See attached for game directions.

Activity 4 (3 minutes)

Play *Teléfono*. Teacher chooses a number word to whisper into the student's ear. Students pass the word around the circle. The last person to hear the word says it aloud. This is a good closing activity appropriate to use after a more excitable game like Box Toss.

Closure

Say goodbye to the class in the target language. **Adiós, clase!**

Box Toss Game

Buy a large postal box. Cover the box with clear contact paper. Use wall mount tabs to adhere number cards to each side of the box.

To play the game, ask each student what number might come face up when the box is thrown into the air. After each student has a turn to guess a number, teacher throws the box into the air on the count of three. Students who have guessed the number that comes face up will cheer!

Diez Deditos

Dos manitos, diez deditos,

Dos manitos, diez deditos,

Dos manitos, diez deditos,

Cúentalos conmigo.

Uno, dos, tres, deditos,

Cuatro, cinco, seis deditos,

Siete, ocho, nueve deditos,

Y uno más son diez.

Resources

Kratky, Lada Josefa. *Somos Amigos*. 1995. Carmel, CA: Hampton Brown Books.

Orozco, Jose. *Diez Deditos/Ten Little Fingers*. 1985. Berkley, CA: Arco Iris Records.

Third Grade French Lesson
Prepared by Eglal Nasser, Syosset Schools

The following lesson plan is the second lesson plan designed for a unit composed of 7 classes. Each class meets on a 6-day cycle for 50 minutes. Each class has approximately 21 children, ranging in age from 7 to 10. The classes incorporate drawing and food activities. Activities are conducted in French.

Objectives

Children will be able to do the following:
* Sing "Sur le Pont d'Avignon"
* Recite the comptine "Il pleut, il mouille"
* Count from 6 to 10
* Respond to the question "Comment tu t'appelles" and give their French name
* Identify the words girl and boy
* Learn vocabulary related to parts of the apple
* Identify the color red

Materials

Red apples - a cutting board - a knife - red napkins

Hand out: a grid to draw the apple - crayons

Puppets: a frog and a dog

Vocabulary

*Une pomme rouge   *Je mange une pomme   *Je dessine une pomme

Activity 1

The teacher circulates and shakes hand with each student saying:

"Bonjour! Comment tu t'appelles? Tu es une fille ou un garçon?"

Activity 2

Puppet show - Les marionettes

Gribouille la grenouille et Lucien le chien

G   Bonjour! je m'appelle Gribouille.

L   Bonjour! je m'appelle Lucien

G   Tu es une fille?

L   Non!

G   Tu es un garçon?

L   Non! Non!

G   Alors?

L   Je suis un chien! Ouaf! Ouaf!

G   Ah!

L   Tu es une fille?

G   Non!

L   Tu es un garçon?

G   Non! Non!

L   Alors?

G   Je suis une grenouille! Croak! Croak!

L   Je m'appelle Lucien, je suis un chien. Ouaf! Ouaf!

G   Je m'appelle Gribouille, je suis une grenouille. Croak! Croak

G & L Et nous sommes des amis!

Activity 3

The teacher will review numbers from 0 to 5 by having the children repeat after her and by writing numbers on the board and having children identify them in French. The teacher will say the numbers 6 to 10 and have children repeat. The teacher will count again and have the children repeat. The teacher will count down and have the children repeat.

Activity 4

The teacher will show an apple, and teach the word "pomme" and say "Repetez."

The teacher will say, "une pomme rouge" and show red things in the classroom repeating the word rouge. Repetez: "Rouge."

The teacher will show the apple and repeat "Une pomme rouge" and ask the children to repeat.

The teacher will cut the apple and show the different parts. The children will repeat after the teacher.

"La peau, la chair, les pépins." Each child will be given an apple, a grid, and crayons.

The teacher will explain to the children that they have to draw the apple, eat the apple and draw the apple, and repeat the activity until they finish the apple and draw what is left. They will then count the "pépins."

The teacher will collect the grid and children will be free to take the seeds home to plant them.

Activity 5

The children will stand up and sing "Sur le Pont d'Avignon"

The children will recite the comptine "Il pleut"

Closure

The teacher will review the new vocabulary.

Thank the children for their attention and praise them for their behavior.

Say "Au revoir," thank the classroom teacher by saying "Merci Madame," and of course give her an apple.

Fifth Grade Latin Lesson
Prepared by Diane McLoughlin, Syosset Schools

Objective

Students will be able to identify ancient Roman and Greek gods, heroes, and themes in actual works of art based on prior study of the subject.

Materials needed

1. Various pictures of paintings, sculptures and statues easily obtained through the Internet. Various time periods would be ideal, and multiple time periods of the same subject are also key.

2. Pictures should be blown up to 8" by 11" (transfer them to a Publisher *Page* and enlarge), laminated and numbered.

3. Tape or tacks to hang the pictures around the room, transforming it into a museum or art gallery.

4. Worksheets of numbered lines for students' notes and identification of the numbered pictures.

Anticipatory Set

Students should be led into a museum atmosphere. Tell them of the expected behaviors at such a place. Tell them how to view the subjects (i.e. study the picture, let your mind go, think of stories, discuss the picture with a classmate if necessary, etc). Tell them they do not need to go in order, to wander about at their leisure. It is not the point to get the "answers" as quickly as possible, etc.

Warm-up

Show students some examples of the artwork and discuss them together.

Activity 1 **(15-20 minutes, depending on number of pictures)**

Students move about the classroom with their worksheet looking at the pictures. Students may share ideas or work alone. Students will take notes and write down who the god or hero is or what the theme is.

Activity 2 (15-20 minutes)

Discuss many or all of the pictures and elicit from the students what their conclusions are and what led them to their conclusions. What "clues" helped them identify the subject.

Closure

Debrief students on how it felt being "in" a museum and being a knowledgeable patron. Assure students that they will be seeing these subjects and using these "museum skills" in the future. Assure students that they will encounter these works of art and many others dealing with ancient Greece and Rome in the future.

Possible follow up

Identify the famous or well-known paintings. Give the artists' names, the name of a painting, when and where it was painted and what museum it is displayed in.

Third Grade Italian Lesson
Prepared by Josephine A. Maietta, Syosset Schools

Objective

To use the high quality song "Santa Lucia" and to challenge students to "think poetically" while understanding the life and culture of the people living in the harbor of Santa Lucia (Napoli).

Materials

Tape recorder, cassette, video, map of Italy, flags, props for Santa Lucia, construction paper, crayons.

Vocabulary

Santa Lucia, mare, luccica, astro d'argento (luna), barchetta, vento

Presentation

Students will hear the song Santa Lucia. While they are listening to the song from the cassette, the teacher will explain the song by using TPR and pointing to the props created. The teacher will sing the song, again pointing to the props.

The teacher will model pronunciation of new words, allowing time for repetition.

The teacher will then sing a section at a time and students will repeat several times. The song will be fun because the students will sing and act it out too.

Warm up

Review of previous lesson. To conclude the warm up, the teacher will ask the students, What is the capital of Italy? A student will respond: Roma. A student will place a little Italian flag on the map. Where is Roma? The teacher will tell the students that not too far from Roma there is another beautiful city near the ocean called Napoli and in the Bay of Napoli there is a harbor called Santa Lucia.

Activity 1

The students will recite the song to master correct pronunciation several times.

Activity 2

The students seated at their seats will act as sailboats and sing the song.

Activity 3

The students will stand up and squat down gently while singing the song, giving the impression that their sailboats are moving.

Activity 4

The students will be recorded as they are singing and then they will listen to the recording and make the necessary corrections.

Activity 5

The students will turn to the page in their books and read about the harbor of Santa Lucia and why it is famous.

Activity 6

The students will also read the lyrics in the book. The students will sing the lyrics. The teacher will then turn off the lights in the classroom, leaving only one on to represent the moon shining on the sea. All the students seated in their seats will row their imaginary sailboats, believing to be in the Bay of Napoli and they will sing the song, Santa Lucia.

Activity 7

The students will color the little sailboat in the book adding all the necessary elements to make the little sailboat look as described by the song.

Activity 8

As a culminating activity, the students will create a quilt. The teacher will give each student a piece of construction paper (8x10). Each student will have to draw and color something pertaining to the song and its features. For example, a student may choose to draw a sailboat and the ocean. She may want to write the word in Italian. Another student may draw the bay with restaurants and write a line from the song, etc. Then put all the pieces together and hang the quilt. It will make a great conversation piece, or display for the building.

Closure

Briefly talk about their reactions and feelings to the song. Students will also view a short segment from the video "Touring Italy" and see first hand what the Bay of Napoli looks like in real life and place a little Italian flag on the map of Italy, exactly where Napoli is located.

Homework

Continue greeting your family and friends in Italian and sing the song Santa Lucia to your family.

This lesson plan can be completed in three half hour lessons or in a completed lesson of a block schedule.

Appendix O

Sample Proposal for a Sequential FLES Program

<u>LAWRENCE PUBLIC SCHOOLS</u>

FOREIGN LANGUAGE IN THE

ELEMENTARY SCHOOLS

REPORT AND

RECOMMENDATIONS

MAY 1999

Dr. Paul Kelleher,

Superintendent of Schools

Lawrence Public Schools

District Central Offices

P.O. Box 477

Lawrence, New York 11559

(516) 295-8000

Reprinted with Permission

INTRODUCTION

This report results from three months of work by a committed, hard-working group of teachers, parents, and administrators. The full Committee met on a weekly basis during this period to fulfill its charge. In addition to the meetings, individuals and sub-groups; gathered and shared research, visited existing elementary second language programs, and talked with experts in the field.

In the course of its work, the Committee identified essential features of a high quality program. These include:

- Clear goals that embrace both high expectations for the development of language skills, as well as the growth of cultural awareness;

- Literacy connections between second languages and classroom teachers; and,

- Strong parental involvement and support.

The proposal that follows attempts to integrate these features into the program philosophy and design.

EXECUTIVE SUMMARY

- The Lawrence elementary second language program in Spanish, beginning in kindergarten next year will provide both language proficiency and cultural awareness to students by the end of their 8th grade study. As defined in the report, *"Proficiency is the ability to effectively communicate in a second language with a native speaker in real-life situations."*

- Implementation of the program will be phased-in, beginning in kindergarten next year and adding a grade each year. This careful approach will allow us to learn from our experience and develop our organizational capacity to insure effective implementation. Phased-in implementation will also diffuse the impact on the budget of the increased program cost.

- Summer curriculum work each year will focus on the development of learning objectives and knowledge and skill outcomes for student by grade level. Both primary and supplementary instructional materials will also be developed.

- Lawrence's elementary second language program in Spanish will be an additional academic subject for each student.

- Classroom teachers and Spanish teachers will be partners in order to reinforce the literacy learning connections with other language learning experiences. Instruction by the Spanish teacher will occur in the regular classroom with the classroom teacher present either tow or three periods per week, depending on the grade level. At least one or two periods per week, depending on the grade level, the classroom teacher will reinforce language learning through videotapes or other supplementary materials.

- Effective elementary second language teachers will require knowledge and skills in both early childhood education and Spanish. These positions will require either a combination of elementary education and a bilingual certificate or a secondary Spanish certificate with an elementary extension.

- Staff development for both classroom teachers and elementary Spanish teachers will be of critical importance. Regular time for communication and coordination will also be important to build into our school schedules.

- A systematic program of parent communication, including informational letters and presentations prior to the program beginning each year, will occur.

- Both student and program assessment will be ongoing and continuous. Formal program assessment reports will be presented at least annually.

- The estimated cost of the program will be approximately $70,000 in the first year and will rise to an annual cost of $750,000 by the end of the sixth year when the program is fully implemented in all schools in grades K-5.

FLES STUDY GROUP MEMBERSHIP

Gerry Wolf – Chairperson of Second Language Department

and Study Group Chairperson

Anette Ramos – Grade 1 Teacher, Number One School

Luz Hernandez-Lee – ESL Teacher, Number Two School

Heather Hudson – ESL Teacher, Number Four School

Yvonne Nicholas – Principal, Number Four School

Jerry Goldsmith – Principal, Number Five School

Liz Ropers – Grade 1 Teacher, Number Five School

Linda Pawlak – ESL Teacher, Number Six School

Myra Delegianis – Spanish Teacher, Lawrence Middle School

Alice Lane – Grade 6 Teacher, Lawrence Middle School

Andrew Livanis – Psychologist, Lawrence Middle School

Jeannine Avallone – Spanish Teacher, Lawrence High School

Dyan Zeller Harris – Supervisor of Community Services

Donna DeLucia -Troisi – Coordinator of Instruction

Kathy Raquet-Barry – Central Council PTA

Gloria Richter – Central Council PTA

Mark Rosenbaum – Assistant Superintendent for Curriculum

Paul Kelleher – Superintendent of Schools

FLES PHILOSOPHY STATEMENT

Lawrence Public Schools envisions a future in which all students are prepared with the knowledge and skills to live and prosper in our global community.

In order to empower students to live fully and work effectively in our inter-connected and diverse world, the Lawrence Public Schools has organized a program of Foreign Language in the Elementary Schools (FLES). *The exquisite connection between the culture that is lived and the language that is spoken can only be realized by those who possess the knowledge of both* (Standards for Foreign Language Learning: Preparing for the 21st Century, 1996).

The FLES Program will enable students to acquire language skills essential to language proficiency and will foster the development of higher-order thinking skills, encourage divergent thinking, and stimulate the creativity of all students.

PROGRAM GOALS

- To teach all students to communicate beyond their native language so that they can participate effectively in the world.

- To establish standards consistent with those set by New York State.

  Standard 1: Students will be able to use a language other than English for Communication.

  Standard 2: Students will develop cross-cultural skills and understanding.

Proficiency is the ability to effectively communicate in a second language with a native speaker in real-life situations. It is the ability to socialize, provide and acquire information, express personal feelings and opinions, and get others to adopt a course of action.

Proficiency enhances the likelihood that students will attain fluency in the future. The acquisition of language develops along a continuum, therefore it occurs over time. The integration of meaningful second language experiences and expressive opportunities will increase the chances of fluency. Fluency will fluctuate based on the degree of exposure (Curtain & Pesola, 1994; Lipton, 1998; Rosenbusch, 1995).

- To enable students to recognize that which is common to all human experience and to accept that which is different.

- To enhance students' abilities to analyze, compare and contrast, synthesize, improvise, and examine cultures through a language and perspective other than their own.

- To begin language study as early as possible in an interdisciplinary environment in which all students are included.

RATIONALE

I. The study of a second language will enhance learning in other areas of study, including reading, listening skills, social studies, and mathematics. It does not come at the expense of basic skills (Armstrong & Rogers, 1997; Curtain, 1998; Donoghue, 1967; Day & Simpson, 1996; Garfinkel & Tabor, 1991; Masciantonio, 1977; National Committee for Latin & Greek, 1995; Rafferty, 1986; Ratte, 1988; Thomas, Collier, & Abbott, 1993).

II. The study of a second language will help students develop a clearer understanding of the English language and greater sensitivity to structure, vocabulary and syntax (Bialystock, 1997; Barik & Swain, 1975; DeLorenzo & Gladstein, 1984; Genesee, 1987; Harley, 1986; Holobow, 1987; Larkin, 1990; Rosenbusch, 1995; Snow, 1990; Swain, 1981).

III. The study of a second language will help students develop a greater awareness of and deeper understanding of other cultures and increases the likelihood of their developing more interactions with persons from other nations (Curtain, 1987; Curtain & Pesola, 1989; Met, 1991; National Standards in Foreign Language Education, 1995; President's Commission on Foreign Languages and International Studies, 1979; Riestra & Johnson, 1964).

IV. The study of a second language will help students to earn higher SAT scores, especially in verbal areas (College Board, 1982, 1992; Cooper, 1987; Eddy, 1981; Solomon, 1984; Weather ford, 1986).

V. The study of a foreign language at an early age will provide greater opportunity for the development of proficiency and fluency. Young children are naturally curious and developmentally ready to learn (American Council on Education Commission on

242

International Education, 1989; Black, 1993; Carnegie Foundation for the Advancement of Teaching, 1983;Curtain, 1993; Hancock, 1996; Izzo, 1981; Lach, 1997; Lambert & Klineberg, 1967; Lee, 1977; Macaulay, 1980; Met & Rhodes, 1990; Nash, 1997; Oyama, 1976; President's Commission on Foreign Languages and International Studies, 1979; Rafferty, 1986; Schumann, 1975; Sparkman, 1966).

VI. The study of a foreign language in the elementary grades places it in its proper place as one of the core academic subjects (Goals 2000: The Educate America Act, 1994; National Association of Elementary School Principals, 1987; National Association of State Boards of Education, 1988; National Commission on Excellence in Education, 1983; National Council of State Supervisors of Foreign Languages, 1989; National Governors' Association, 1990).

VII. The study of a foreign language will enhance the future employability of students (College Board, 1983; Curtain, 1993; Met, 1989; Villano, 1996).

The study of a foreign language will enable students to develop: more flexibility in thinking processes through problem solving, conceptualizing and reasoning; improved memory; greater analytic and interpretive capacities; greater creativity; and, divergent thinking capacity (Bamford, 1989; Bamford & Mizokawa, 1991; Ben Zeev, 1977; Bruck, Lambert, & Tucker, 1974; Foster & Reeves, 1989; Lambert, 1981; Landry, 1973; Makuta, 1984, 1986; Met, 1989, 1991; Peal & Lambert, 1962; Rosenbusch, 1995; Weatherford, 1986).

VIII.   The early study of foreign language facilitates the learning of additional foreign languages (Lipton, 1992).

IX. The choice of Spanish as the second language to be learned in elementary school will enhance the opportunities for our students to thrive in an increasingly multilingual society (Curtain, 1989).

X. Additional claims stated in professional journal articles, but not supported by specific research citations, include: enhanced performance on entrance exams such as ACTs, MCATs, and LSATs; enhanced self-esteem; increased appreciation for the aesthetics of literature, music and art; improved knowledge of geography; greater opportunity for career exploration; greater likelihood of earning college credits while in high school; and, increased opportunities to conduct research and/or study in a foreign country.

CURRICULUM DEVELOPMENT FOR THE FLES PROGRAM

I.   A FLES Steering Committee will be formed to provide on-going planning, coordination and support for the program. The Steering Committee will be comprised of representatives from the stakeholder groups. Curriculum development will be a responsibility of appropriate staff members.

II.   Summer curriculum writing projects each year will focus on the development of learning objectives and outcomes by grade level. Language skills on an appropriate communicative level will be integrated with grade level content.

III.   Development of a resource guide for the purpose of reinforcement by the classroom teacher, to include available trade books, audio-visual, technology, software, etc., will be part of each grade level project.

IV.   Evaluation and modifications of existing curriculum for each grade level will be based on the results of annual program assessment.

STAFF DEVELOPMENT FOR FLES PROGRAM

The Lawrence Public Schools will provide the resources needed to empower classroom teachers to successfully implement the FLES Program. It is our expectation that all affected staff members (which could include administrators, aides, support staff, specialists and others) will participate in a variety of these opportunities in order to attain the skills and knowledge needed to provide the reinforcement activities required by the program design.

Staff Development Days

September – introductory workshops will be provided to teachers involved in the program for the first time by building or grade level.

November/March – workshops for teachers presently involved in the program as well as introduction workshops for teachers who will be involved in the program for the following year (building and/or district), will be provided.

Contractual Meeting Time (Tuesday afternoon and Grade Level Meetings)

On-going workshops for teachers involved in the program, as well as for teachers who will be involved in the future, will be offered in each school.

District In-service Program/Summer In-service

Workshops will be offered to all staff members presently involved in the program, as well as for teachers who will be involved in future years. In-service courses will include, but not limited to:

Introduction to Spanish

How to Integrate a Second Language into Your Classroom

Course Offerings by Outside Agencies

Courses related to the FLES Program offered by outside agencies, universities and other school districts will be made available to our teachers for in-service or graduate credit, where appropriate.

Support by FLES Teacher(s)

The FLES teacher(s) will provide formal and informal support to classroom and special area teachers in a variety of settings (i.e. prep periods, congruent periods).

FLES INSTRUCTIONAL TIME ALLOCATIONS

Kindergarten   Direct instruction by the FLES teacher – 20 minutes, 3x per week

Reinforcement by the Classroom teacher – one 20-minute session per week in a Spanish Lab "Nuestra Casa."

Classroom experience in the Spanish Learning Center. Listening Center, Computer Center, and Library.

Integration of language and cultural skills with art, music, and physical education programs.

The FLES Program on the elementary level builds upon the kindergarten design by adding increased reinforcement by the classroom teacher in grades one and two and by increasing all instructional time allotments in grades three, four and five.

Grades One and Two

Direct Instruction by the FLES teacher – 20 minutes, 3x per week

Reinforcement by the classroom teacher – 20 minutes, 2x per week

Grades Three, Four, And Five

Direct Instruction by the FLES teacher – 45 minutes, 2x per week

Reinforcement by the classroom teacher – 45 minutes, 1x per week

Reinforcement experiences may include the use of videos, computer software, classroom learning centers, books on tapes, art, music, and a variety of literary activities.

PROGRAM DESIGN

I.   The Program will utilize the FLES design, not FLEX.

    A.   FLES refers to Foreign Language in the Elementary School. This model provides sequential foreign language instruction for two or more years. The program goals are centered on language proficiency and cultural awareness. Contact times are 2-5 times per week for a minimum of 60 minutes per week (5-15% of the day), depending on the grade level.

    B.   FLES refers to Foreign Language Exploration or Experience, which offers two or more languages with a focus on cultural awareness. Language experiences are offered 1-3 times per week for 20-35 minutes per week (1-5% of the day). There is less time for the development of language skills.

II.   The FLES program will use an interdisciplinary approach to language learning and will be content and skills based.

III. The Program will begin by introducing Spanish instruction next year in kindergarten. Each succeeding year one new grade will be added. The spiral approach integrates new knowledge and skills with prior learning.

IV.   The FLES Program will use a "push-in" model. The language specialist will come to the regular teacher's classroom to provide the Spanish lessons. The classroom teacher will be present and involved to enable him/her to reinforce the learning and become increasingly more capable of modeling and reviewing concepts and vocabulary.

V. Common planning time will be incorporated into the school program to enable the classroom teacher and the language specialist appropriate time to develop content-based activities.

VI. A sample program schedule follows:

KINDERGARTEN FLES SCHEDULE

TIME	MONDAY	TUESDAY	WESDNES DAY	THURSDAY	FRIDAY
9:20-9:45 a.m.	Bldg. Resource	Bldg. Resource	Bldg. Resource	Bldg. Resource	Bldg. Resource
9:45-10:05 a.m.	Teacher 1	Teacher 1	Teacher 2	Teacher 1	Articulation
10:10-10:30 a.m.	Teacher 3	Teacher 2	Teacher 3	Teacher 3	Meetings with
10:35-10:55 a.m.	Teacher 5	Teacher 4	Teacher 4	Teacher 5	Teaching staff
11:00-11:20 a.m.	Teacher 6	Teacher 6	Teacher 7	Teacher 6	Curriculum Review
11:25-11:45 a.m.	Teacher 8	Teacher 7	Teacher 8	Teacher 9	Materials
11:50-12:10 p.m.	Teacher 9	Teacher 10	Teacher 9	Teacher 10	Selection
12:10-1:00 p.m.	Lunch	Lunch	Lunch	Lunch	Lunch
1:00-1:20 p.m.	Teacher 11	Teacher 12	Teacher 11	Teacher 12	Articulation
1:25-1:45 p.m.	Teacher12	Teacher 13	Teacher 10	Teacher 13	Meetings with
1:50-2:10 p.m.	Teacher 2	Teacher 5	Teacher 13	Teacher 4	Teaching staff
2:15-2:35 p.m.	Teacher 7	Teacher 8	Bldg. Resource	Teacher 11	Bldg. Resource
2:40-3:20 p.m.	PREP	PREP	PREP	PREP	PREP

PARENT/COMMUNITY INVOLVEMENT

- An informational letter will be sent out to our parents and community outlining the pilot FLES Program.

- The parents and community will be invited to a presentation regarding the pilot FLES Program.

- The FLES teacher will provide regular communication to parents regarding the FLES Program and school and classroom activities. Lists of support materials that can be used at home (CD-Rom, video, and reading materials) will be made available to parents.

- Parent workshops will be made available to enable parents to incorporate learning strategies into their children's educational experience.

- Parents will meet with the FLES teacher on Back to School Night.

- An outreach program to the Hispanic community, inviting them to participate in programs of cultural topics relating to their authentic experiences, will be initiated.

- A FLES community bulletin board to announce student/parent activities will be created in each school.

ASSESSMENT

The FLES Program and the achievement of students will be assessed annually, based on expectations established in the New York State Learning Standards.

Standard 1 Communication Skills

Listening and speaking are primary communicative goals in modern language learning. These skills are used for the purposes of socializing, providing and acquiring information, expressing personal feelings and opinions, and getting others to adopt a course of action.

Students can:

- Comprehend language consisting of simple vocabulary and structures in fact-to-face conversation with peers and familiar adults

- Comprehend the main idea of more extended conversations with some unfamiliar vocabulary and structures as well as cognates of English words

- Call upon repetition, rephrasing, and nonverbal cues to derive or convey meaning from a language other than English

- Use appropriate strategies to initiate and engage in simple conversations with more fluent or native speakers of the same age group, familiar adults, and providers of common public services.

This is evident, for example, when students:

- Exchange simple greetings and answer questions about self and family

- Listen to radio broadcasts and answer questions about main ideas

- Speak in complete sentences, using present tense and, occasionally, markers for past and future tenses

- Ask for information or directions

- Discuss classroom activities with a peer

- Use appropriate body language and gestures to supplement the spoken word.

Standard 2 Cultural Understanding

Effective communication involves meanings that go beyond words and require and understanding of perceptions, gestures, folklore, and family and community dynamics. All of these elements can affect whether and how well a message is received.

Students can:

- Use some key cultural traits of the societies in which the target language is spoken.

This is evident, for example, when students:

- Recognize cultural patterns and traditions of the target cultures in the target language;

- Understand the cultural implications of the spoken language and the dynamics of social interaction; and

- Correctly use and interpret cultural manifestations, such as gestures accompanying greeting and leave taking and the appropriate distance to maintain.

The FLES teacher and the classroom teacher will evaluate student progress. A progress report will be given to parents reflecting performance on a continuum of language development, along with a rating for participation. As part of our summer curriculum development process, rubrics will be developed to measure student growth in each of the key goal areas.

In addition, questionnaires will be provided to students, parents, teachers and administrators to obtain feedback about the FLES Program near the end of each school year, beginning in kindergarten. In the first year of implementation a pre-program survey will be given to the teachers and parents of incoming kindergarten students, following the initial orientation programs. The purpose will be to determine teacher and parent attitudes about the value of foreign language instruction, the importance of learning about different cultures, etc. The end-of-year survey will then allow us to measure any observable changes in attitude over time.

1999 FLES PROGRAM IMPLEMENTATION SCHEDULE

ACTIVITY	TIME	PERSON RESPONSIBLE
Job Announcement Posted	Immediately	Personnel Office
Screening of Applicants	Mid-June	Committee
Hire Teacher	June	Committee/Board
Visitation – Oceanside	June	#4 School Teachers
Organize Curriculum Writing Project	June	Assistant Superintendent
Curriculum Writing	July-Mid-August	FLES Teacher and #4 School Teachers
Order Materials	Mid-August	#4 School Staff
Introductory Workshop For Kindergarten Teachers	September	FLES Teacher and #4 School Principal
Establish In-service Program	October	Coordinator of Title I
Staff Development Day Workshops	November	Coordinator of Instruction and Staff Development Day Committee
Staff Development Day Workshops	March	Coordinator of Instruction and Staff Development Day Committee

IMPACT ANALYSIS

The introduction of the FLES program in Kindergarten in September, 1999 represents only the first step in a multi-year implementation process that will affect future staffing and budgets. This analysis estimates impacts in both areas. The costs presented depend on several assumptions. First, projected enrollments assume recent trends in overall elementary enrollment and the distribution of that enrollment by school will continue for the next five years. Actual variances from these projections will, of course, affect both staffing and budget costs. Second, at grade levels where projected enrollments are near "breakpoints," this analysis conservatively chooses the higher number of sections. In all likelihood, therefore, unless an unforeseen enrollment increase occurs, the actual number of classes and the staffing required should be somewhat lower than estimates. Third, staffing projections assume an average staffing load of 200 minutes per day (5 periods X 40 minutes) for each full-time second language teacher – including both instructional and collaborative planning time. The fact that instructional delivery in this program does not fit existing time patterns complicates these estimates. The fact that in most schools in most years part-time teachers will be required further complicates them, since travel time will effectively reduce available instructional time. Ultimately, staffing load will have to be negotiated with the LTA.

This chart below summarizes five-year impacts on staff and budget. The detailed analysis follows:

YEAR	NUMBER OF TEACHERS	TOTAL BUDGET ESTIMATE
1999 – 00	1.0	$ 72,000
2000 – 01	2.8	$212,960
2001 – 02	4.6	$335,720
2002 – 03	6.6	$472,120
2003 – 04	9.0	$635,800
2004 – 05	10.7	$751,740

ELEMENTARY LANGUAGE SUMMARY OF BUDGET PROJECTION

2004-05	# OF TEACHERS		COST	TOTALS
	10.7	Salaries	$ 600,270	
		Benefits	$ 129,470	
		Equip.		
		Supplies	$ 6,000	
		Instruct. Materials	$ 10,000	
		Training	$ 6,000	
				$ 751,740

PROJECTED ENROLLMENT AND NUMBER OF SECTIONS

	1999-00	2000-01	2001-02	2002-03	2003-04	20004-05
K Enrollment	250	240	240	240	240	240
# of Sections	13	13	13	13	13	13
Number One						
Grade 1 Enroll		57	55	55	55	55
# Cl.		3	3	3	3	3
Grade 2 Enroll			52	50	50	50
# Cl.			3	3	3	3
Grade 3 Enroll				59	57	57
# Cl.				3	3	3
Grade 4 Enroll					68	65
# Cl.					4	3-4
Grade 5 Enroll						66
# Cl.						3-4
Number Two						
Grade 1 Enroll	74	80	77	77	77	77
# Cl.	4	4	4	4	4	4
Grade 2 Enroll			87	84	84	84
# Cl.			4-5	4-5	4-5	4-5
Grade 3 Enroll				85	81	81
# Cl.				4	4	4
Grade 4 Enroll					85	82
# Cl.					4-5	4
Grade 5 Enroll						76
# Cl.						4
Number Five						
Grade 1 Enroll	61	65	63	63	63	63
# Cl.	3	3-4	3-4	3-4	3	3
Grade 2 Enroll			68	65	65	65
# Cl.			4	3-4	3-4	3-4
Grade 3 Enroll				55	53	53
# Cl.				3	3	3
Grade 4 Enroll					56	54
# Cl.					4	3
Grade 5 Enroll						61
# Cl.						3
Number Six						
Grade 1 Enroll	56	60	58	58	58	58
# Cl.	3	3	3	3	3	3
Grade 2 Enroll			52	50	50	50
# Cl.			3	3	3	3
Grade 3 Enroll				54	52	52
# Cl.				3	3	3
Grade 4 Enroll					52	50
# Cl.					3	3
Grade 5 Enroll						58
# Cl.						3
Total K	13	13	13	13	13	13
Total 1st		13-14	13-14	13-14	13	13
Total 2nd			14-15	13-14	13-15	13-15
Total 3rd				13	13	13
Total 4th					15-16	13-15
Total 5th						13-14
Grand Total	13	26-27	40-42	52-54	67-70	78-83

ELEMENTARY LANGUAGE FIVE -YEAR BUDGET PROJECTION

1999-00	# OF TEACHERS		COST	TOTALS
	FTE			
	1.0	Salaries	$ 55,000	
		Benefits	$ 11,000	
		Equip.		
		Supplies	$ 1,500	
		Instruct. Materials	$ 3,000	
		Training	$ 1,500	
				$ 72,000

2000-01	# OF TEACHERS		COST	TOTALS
	2.8	Salaries	$ 157,080	
		Benefits	$ 33,880	
		Equip.		
		Supplies	$ 6,000	
		Instruct. Materials	$ 10,000	
		Training	$ 6,000	
				$ 212,960

2001-02	# OF TEACHERS		COST	TOTALS
	4.6	Salaries	$ 258,060	
		Benefits	$ 55,660	
		Equip.		
		Supplies	$ 6,000	
		Instruct. Materials	$ 10,000	
		Training	$ 6,000	
				$ 335,720

2002-03	# OF TEACHERS		COST	TOTALS
	6.6	Salaries	$ 370,260	
		Benefits	$ 79,860	
		Equip.		
		Supplies	$ 6,000	
		Instruct. Materials	$ 10,000	
		Training	$ 6,000	
				$ 472,120

2003-04	# OF TEACHERS			COST		TOTALS	
	9.0	Salaries		$	504,900		
		Benefits		$	108,900		
		Equip.					
		Supplies		$	6,000		
		Instruct. Materials		$	10,000		
		Training		$	6,000		
						$	635,800

ADDITIONAL IMPACT CONSIDERATIONS

As previously described, the phase-in of the new elementary second language program begins with the kindergarten class of September 1999. At the same time, we want to provide opportunities for students at other grade levels to begin to experience the value of second language learning. Towards that end, we are recommending that a second language component be added for grades one through five utilizing the following vehicles:

(1)After School Enrichment Programs,

(2) Super Saturday Program,

(3) Classroom Enrichment.

The classroom enrichment component would involve some introductory lessons in the Spanish language utilizing software, video and audio resources, along with cultural awareness activities using these resources, enhanced by literature to be made available in our classroom and school libraries. In the second year of the program, when FLES teachers will be present in each of the five elementary schools, we will be able to expand these opportunities.

It is anticipated that these additional activities will provide every elementary student with some exposure to second language learning throughout the phase-in process, while staying within the parameters of the budget outlined in this report.

SITE VISITS CONDUCTED

Site visits were conducted by 3 or 4 members of the FLES committee on the dates shown below. The results of the visits were then shared with the full committee.

1. Roslyn Heights Elementary School   February 23, 1999

2. Southampton Elementary School   February 23, 1999

3. Oceanside School #6   February 24, 1999

4. Westhampton Beach Elementary School   March 5, 1999

In addition, a team of staff members from #4 School visited the Oceanside Kindergarten Center to observe their K-FLES program on May 11, 1999.

FLES RESEARCH, JOURNAL ARTICLES, PUBLICATIONS REVIEWED

Armstrong, Kimberly M. Yetter-Vassot, Cindy, *Transforming Teaching through Technology,* Foreign Language Annals, 1994

Black, Susan, *Learning Languages,* The Executive Educator, 1993

Brown, R., *Toward and Interactional Approach:* A Theoretical Perspective, 1987

Bruno, Linda; Betts, Jacque; Kriss, Steve; Byrnes, Rita; Meyers, Cherie; Miller, Donna;

Weinman, Betsy; *Proposal on Foreign Language in the Elementary School,* Oceanside Schools, 1998Chavez, Carmen L., *Students Take Flight with*

Daedalus: Learning Spanish in a Networked Classroom, Foreign Language Annuals, 1997

Curtain, Helena, *Methods in Elementary School Foreign Language Teaching,* Foreign Language Annals, 1991

Ganschow, Leonore; Sparks, Richard L.; Javorsky, James, *Foreign Language Learning Difficulties: A Historical Perspective,* Journal of Learning Disabilities, 1998

Garcia, Paul A. and Gramer, Virginia, *On Implementing an Elementary School Language Program Reflections and Considerations,* 1998.

Garfinkel, Alan and Tabor, Kenneth, *Elementary School Foreign Languages and English Reading Achievement: A New View of the Relationship,* Foreign Language Annals, 1991.

Ging, Diane F., *Teaching Critical Languages in Public Schools,* Theory into Practice, 1994

Glisan, Eileen W.; Dudt, Kurt P.; Howe, Marilyn S., *Teaching Spanish Through Distance Education Implications of a Pilot Study,* Foreign Language Annals, 1998

Hammond, Jan, *Teaching Foreign Language in the Elementary School to Support Literacy,* 1998

Heining-Boynton, Audrey, *Early Childhood Foreign Language Education: Developmental Perspective and Implementation Guidelines,* Kappa Delta Pi Record, 1992

Lipton, Gladys, *What Strategies are Useful When Advocating for the Initiation of Program?,* 1998

Margarita, Elaine, *FLES Programs on Long Island,* 1999

Met, Myriam, *Learning Language through Content: Learning Content through Language,* Foreign Language Annals, 1991

Moeller, Aleidine, *Content-Based Foreign Language Instruction in the Middle School: An Experiential Learning Approach,* Foreign Language Annals, 1994

Moeller, Aleidine J., and Sullivan Scott, Elizabeth, *Making the Match: Middle Level Goals and Foreign Language Instruction,* Schools in the Middle, 1993

Overfield, Denise M., *From the Margins to the Mainstream: Foreign Language Education and Community Based Learning,* Foreign Language Annals, 1997

Pitkoff, Evan and Rosen, Elizabeth, *New Technology, New Attitudes Provide Language Instruction,* NASSP Bulletin, 1994

Redmond, Mary Lynn, *The Whole Language Approach in the FLES Classroom: Adapting Strategies, Teach Reading and Writing,* Foreign Language Annals, 1994

Rhodes, Nancy; Thompson, Lynn and Snow, Marguerite Ann, *A Comparison of FLES and Immersion Programs – Final Report,* Center for Language Education and Research Center for Applied Linguistics, 1989

Rieken, Elizabeth; Kerby, Wilson; Mulhern, Frank, *Building Better Bridges: Middle School to High School Articulation in Foreign Language Programs,* Foreign Language Annals, 1996

Sparks, Richard L.; Ganschow, Leonore; Artzer, Marjorie; Patton, John, *Foreign Language Proficiency At-Risk and Not-At-Risk Learners Over 2 Years of Foreign Language Instruction: A Follow-Up Study,* Journal of Learning Disabilities, 1997

Thomas, Wayne P. and Collier, Virginia P., *Two Languages Are Better Than One,* Educational Leadership, 1998

Traphagan, Tomoko Watanabe, *Interviews with Japanese FLES Students: Descriptive Analysis,* Foreign Language Annals, 1997

Various Articles on *What Strategies are Useful When Advocating for the Initiation of Programs?*

FLES RESEARCH, JOURNAL ARTICLES, PUBLICATIONS REVIEWED

INTERNET SOURCES

1. *A National Survey of Foreign Language Instruction in Elementary and Secondary Schools: A Summary Center for Applied Linguistics,* 1998

2. *Announcing the Ñandu Listserv on Early Foreign Language Learning,* Center for Applied Linguistics, 1999

3. Boston, Carol, *Federal Support for Foreign Language Education,* The ERIC Review; 1998

4. Branaman, Lucinda; Rhodes, Nancy and Rennie, Jeanne, *A National Survey of K-12 Foreign Language Education,* The ERIC Review, 1998

5. Curtain, Helena, *How to Start a K-8 Program: Selecting a Language,* 1997

6. Delaware Department of Education, *Foreign Languages Curriculum Framework Content Standards – State of Delaware,* 1997

7. *Developing Language Proficiency and Connecting School to Students' Lives: Two Standards for Effective Teaching,* ERIC Digest, 1998

8. *Fostering Second Language Development in Young Children,* ERIC Digest, 1995

9. Howard, Elizabeth R. and Loeb, Michael, *In Their Own Words: Two-Way Immersion Teachers Talk About Their Professional Experiences,* ERIC Digest, 1998

10. Marcos, Kathleen, *Parent Brochure: Why, How and When Should my Child Learn a Second Language?* Center for Applied Linguistics, 1998

11. Marcos, Kathleen M., *Second Language Learning: Everyone can Benefit,* The ERIC Review, 1998

12. Marcos, Kathleen M., *Starting a Foreign Language Program,* The ERIC Review, 1998

13. *Myths and Misconceptions About Second Language Learning,* ERIC Digest, 1992

14. *Ñanduti: Early Foreign Language Learning,* The National Foreign Language Standards, 1997

15. *New research on Learning Language,* The Sound Beginnings Newsletter, 1997

16. Rosenbusch, *Guidelines for Starting an Elementary School Foreign Language Program,* ERIC Digest, 1995

17. Rosenbusch, Marcia, H., *Ñanduti,* ERIC Digest, 1995

18. *Speak out for Language Learning,* Center for Applied Linguistics

19. *Spotlight on FLES Programs,* Glastonbury, Connecticut, The ERIC Review, 1998

20. Teel, Jean and Smith, Melissa, *Why is the Study of Foreign Language Necessary?* Foreign Languages: Elementary Core Curriculum Guide Preview, 1998

NOTES

NOTES

NOTES

NOTES

Order Form for

Implementing Successful FLES Programs

Mail your order to:

Dr. Elaine Margarita

92 Capitol Avenue

Williston Park, NY 11596-1621

Email request to: etmrpb@yahoo.com

SHIPPING ADDRESS:

Name_____

Address_____

City, State, Zip Code_____

Phone_____

Order Information:

Price: $35.00 per copy (includes delivery)

Check or Postal Money Order--Payable to: Margarita Publications